Shakespeare
THE GLOBE & THE WORLD

S. SCHOENBAUM

Folger Shakespeare Library
Oxford University Press
NEW YORK OXFORD TORONTO MELBOURNE

The Folger Shakespeare Library is administered by the Trustees of Amherst College. O.B. Hardison, Jr., is Director. The Folger gratefully acknowledges the contributions of the following individuals:

PROJECT DIRECTOR: Philip A. Knachel
PROJECT ADMINISTRATOR: Margaret M. Welch
EXHIBITION DESIGNER: Stuart Silver
CONCEPT AND SCENARIO CONSULTANT: George Trescher
CONCEPT AND CONTENT ADVISOR AND CATALOGUE AUTHOR: S. Schoenbaum
BOOK AND MANUSCRIPT CONSULTANT: Elizabeth Niemyer
EXHIBITION GRAPHICS AND CATALOGUE DESIGNER: David Barnett
PUBLICATIONS EDITOR: John F. Andrews
HEAD CONSERVATOR: J. Franklin Mowery
HEAD PHOTOGRAPHER: Horace Groves
EXHIBITION DESIGN ASSOCIATE: Clifford La Fontaine
EXHIBITION GRAPHICS ASSOCIATE: Doris Neulinger
EXHIBITION TEXT: Michael Feingold
CATALOGUE PRODUCTION: Michelle Nahum
CONSERVATION CONSULTANT: Nathan Stolow
AUDIOVISUAL CONSULTANT: Joseph Empsucha
ACADEMIC CONSULTANTS: Charles H. Shattuck, Lacey Baldwin Smith
PHOTOGRAPHERS: Robert Jackson, Rudy Muller
FOLGER CONSULTANTS: James P. Elder, Nati Krivatsy, Lilly Stone Lievsay, Jean Miller, Joan Morrison, Barry Parker, Sandra Powers, Ann Skiff, Leni Spencer, Laetitia Yeandle
FOLGER STAFF: Sarah Barbour, Louise Hayford, Kelly Hubbell, Nancy Kerns, Patricia Senia, Karin Stanford, Elizabeth Walsh
CATALOGUE INDEXER: Ann Hofstra Grogg

Museums participating in the exhibition:
CALIFORNIA ACADEMY OF SCIENCES
    San Francisco (October–December 1979)
WILLIAM ROCKHILL NELSON GALLERY OF ART
    Kansas City (February–May 1980)
MUSEUM OF ART, CARNEGIE INSTITUTE
    Pittsburgh (June–September 1980)
DALLAS MUSEUM OF FINE ARTS
    Dallas (October 1980–January 1981)
HIGH MUSEUM OF ART
    Atlanta (February–April 1981)

Library of Congress Cataloging in Publication Data
Schoenbaum, Samuel, 1927–
    Shakespeare: The Globe and the World.
    Prepared for a Folger Shakespeare Library exhibition held at various institutions Oct. 1979–Oct. 1981.
    Bibliography: p.
    Includes index.
    1. Shakespeare, William, 1564–1616—Exhibitions. 2. Folger Shakespeare Library, Washington, D.C.
I. Folger Shakespeare Library, Washington, D.C.
II. Title.
PR2933.F64S3   822.3'3   79-3075
ISBN 0-19-502645-4
ISBN 0-19-502646-2 pbk.

Printed in the United States of America by Princeton Polychrome Press, Princeton, New Jersey.
Set in ITC Garamond type by Cardinal Type Service, New York City.
Designed by David Barnett.

Table of Contents

Published to accompany a touring exhibition bearing the same title, this book is made possible by grants to the Folger Shakespeare Library from the National Endowment for the Humanities, Metropolitan Life Insurance Company, Exxon Corporation, and the Corporation for Public Broadcasting.

Foreword

A view of the Reading Room of the Folger Shakespeare Library. Designed by Paul Philippe Cret and constructed between 1930 and 1932, the Folger has been cited many times for its architectural distinction and is one of the few modern buildings listed in the National Register of Historic Places.

This book celebrates the glory of Shakespeare. It has grown out of an exhibition of manuscripts, books, and other objects brought together to illuminate Shakespeare and his works, the world of the English Renaissance in which he lived, and the enduring mark he left on his own and later times.

The illustrations in the text derive from rare materials obtained for the occasion from the vaults of the Folger Shakespeare Library in Washington, D.C. Conceived as a memorial to Shakespeare, this magnificent library was a gift to the American people from Henry Clay Folger and his wife Emily Jordan Folger, who erected it in 1932 to house the vast collection of Shakespeareana they had acquired in the course of many years of dedicated and painstaking search. The rare, and in some cases unique, materials which make the Folger the preeminent center for Shakespeare research in the world today still constitute the heart of the Library's collection. During the forty-seven years since the Library's founding, however, it has expanded the range of its holdings to encompass the whole age of Shakespeare and, more generally, the civilization of Western Europe from the Renaissance to the early modern period.

It is appropriate to acknowledge here the great debt owed those who have contributed so much to the original project, especially Margaret Welch, Elizabeth Niemyer, James Elder, and John Andrews of the Folger and Stuart Silver and George Trescher of New York City. It is also a pleasure to thank the inimitable author of the book that marks the occasion. Sam Schoenbaum has provided a narrative of remarkable grace and erudition, reminding us yet once more that, for all the influence the English Renaissance had on Shakespeare's work, he was (as Ben Jonson was the first to observe) "not of an age, but for all time."

Finally, as project director, I must stress that this book could not have been produced without the encouragement and generous assistance afforded by the National Endowment for the Humanities and the three corporate sponsors: Metropolitan Life Insurance Company, Exxon Corporation, and the Corporation for Public Broadcasting.

Philip A. Knachel
Associate Director
Folger Shakespeare Library

Author's Preface

If the splendors of the Folger Shakespeare Library furnish the occasion for this book, they also comprise much of its substance. I refer not only to the illustrations, but to the accompanying text as well. My charge, agreed upon just a year ago, was to create a book rather different from the usual souvenir guide or museum catalogue—a book that would appeal even to those not in a position to view the actual Folger treasures as the exhibition made its stately civic progress from San Francisco to New York. In other words, a work that might stand on its own. I was asked somehow to marry illustrations and text in "a seamless narrative." That phrase has haunted me.

Because the books and documents that are my materials remain stubbornly disparate even while being, in the broadest sense, related to one another, I have found my task a unique authorial challenge. Is a seamless narrative possible when one must shuttle back and forth between the private spheres of a poet's provincial upbringing and Bankside player's life, on the one hand, and the public arena of statecraft, war, and discovery, on the other—the Globe, as it were, and the world? The reader must judge for himself. As for the author, the challenge has been exhilarating. Although a Folger reader for over two decades, I was here given occasion to study many unique items for the first time. Meanwhile, the books and manuscripts already long familiar to me retained their magic; the honeymoon is still on.

In a happy marriage one partner will wish to avoid upstaging the other. Accordingly, I have sought to defer to the illustrations: this book exists for the collection, not the other way round. I have also resisted any temptation to offer original interpretations of my material. That would be inappropriate here, where a thesis cannot be properly argued; and anyway I would be traveling under a false passport were I to assume the identity of an innovative historian. My subject matter includes a range of topics—among others, the fauna and flora of Warwickshire, country sports, the Spanish Armada, and the roles of Elizabeth I, Mary Queen of Scots, James I, and other great historical personages—with respect to which I can claim only amateur status. I am not a technical historian or (for that matter) a naturalist, merely a curious inquirer.

Therefore I have cheerfully ransacked the best books available to me, such as J. E. Neale on Queen Elizabeth and Samuel Eliot Morison on the voyages of exploration. In doing so I have learned much. I regret that the format of this book prohibits documentation of sources, and thus denies me one of the special pleasures of scholarship, which is the acknowledgment of trusted guides. Perhaps, however, the recommended readings at the end of the volume will to a degree remedy this deficiency, for the titles therein listed include those I have found most useful. A few are old enough to suggest that replacement by more up-to-date surveys would not be amiss; but they still hold value. One older compendium by various hands, *Shakespeare's England*, published during the depths of the Great War, remains helpfully informative on a number of aspects of life in the period. Sometimes I have been called upon to retraverse ground previously covered in my biographical studies of Shakespeare. In doing so, I have not tried self-consciously to vary the narrative, although small differences have arisen naturally. The merging of illustrations and text, however, provides an effect different (I trust) from what other books, my own included, have to offer.

A word about procedures. In quotations I have modernized spelling and punctuation, although the original spelling is generally retained in the captions. In quoting from Shakespeare I have used the Peter Alexander edition of *The Complete Works* (London and Glasgow, 1951). The new year during this period began officially on Lady Day, March 25; in deference to customary practice I have revised the year, where appropriate, in citations.

This is the place for a few personal acknowledgments. John Andrews was a wonderfully considerate and painstaking editor. Lacey Baldwin Smith performed a friend's office, as well as a scholar's, by reading the final typescript and making valuable suggestions on points of detail. Elizabeth Niemyer is largely responsible for the selection of books and manuscripts and for the captions. The photographic skills of Horace Groves, Robert Jackson, and Rudy Muller, with the support of Kelly Hubbell, helped make this publication possible. David Barnett has been a patient and resourceful designer. In the Reading Room, Patricia Senia and Elizabeth Walsh—indeed the entire Folger staff—have throughout proved solicitously helpful beyond the call of duty. I am grateful to Shelia Spector for help in tracking down information, checking quotations from printed sources, and correcting galleys. Oscar Commander continued to impart the special wisdom of his example. And finally, I must thank the project coordinator, Margaret Welch, who brought all of the participants—author, Folger staff, books, pictures—together.

My wife was, as ever, a sustaining presence. Were a dedication in order, I would have it read: "For Marilyn, again."

Among other achievements, the Elizabethan Age was one of the great eras of discovery in world history. Readers are now invited to participate in that age by embarking on their own voyage of discovery, a voyage made possible by the treasures of the Folger exhibited in the pages that follow.

S.S., July 18, 1979

QUEEN ELIZABETH AND WILLIAM
SHAKESPEARE, a drawing by David
Hockney, created for SHAKESPEARE:
THE GLOBE AND THE WORLD (1979).

Prologue

Shakespeare lives. To a greater extent than any other writer, he has posthumously forged the creative consciousness of Western man. His language forms part of the texture of our own, so that whether we realize it or not, Shakespeare is always at our tongue's tip as we go about the ordinary business of daily life. When we commend the glass of fashion, lament the law's delay, or reflect that ambition should be made of sterner stuff, when we make a virtue of necessity, pounce at one fell swoop, or are frightened with false fire, when we sagely observe that misery makes strange bedfellows or that if we bait the hook well the fish will bite—on all such occasions, and countless others, we are quoting Shakespeare. Many of us, like the schoolboy described in *As You Like It,* have crept like snails unwillingly to school, where we have submitted to enforced appreciation of one or more of the Shakespeare plays (*Julius Caesar,* say, or *Macbeth* or *Romeo and Juliet*) which, throughout living memory, have been chosen for the cultural improvement of the young. If we are fortunate, Shakespeare has thereafter become our lifelong companion.

The fortunate are numerous. No dramatist, living or dead, has been more frequently reprinted or performed, or translated into a greater variety of languages. A collected edition of Shakespeare is usually the first choice, along with the Bible, of anyone asked to plan his reading matter in the event of shipwreck on a desert island. All thirty-seven plays live in the repertory—even, since the celebrated Peter Brook-Laurence Olivier production, the formerly despised *Titus Andronicus.* As recently as 1977, Shakespeare's vast youthful trilogy on the reign of Henry VI, which some had thought unactable, returned triumphantly to the stage during the Royal Shakespeare Company's season at Stratford-upon-Avon. In London in the same year, that company's *Comedy of Errors,* with music inspired by Shakespeare's dialogue and lyrics lifted from the play, enraptured multitudes, including the very young, and received an award for best musical of the year. At another Stratford, in Ontario, the distinguished troupe that began life a quarter of a century ago under the direction of Tyrone Guthrie makes a festival of each season with its Shakespearean revivals.

In the United States, Shakespeare festivals dot the summer landscape from Alabama and Vermont west to Colorado and Utah, and on to Oregon and the California coast; a few companies, such as the Folger Theatre Group in Washington, D.C., perform the year round. To the true *aficionado,* Odessa is not a city of the Crimea or some file but the site, in west Texas, of the Odessa Shakespeare Festival—mounted in a reconstructed Elizabethan playhouse called, grandly, the Globe of the Great Southwest. Meanwhile, throughout the school year, campus productions are regular features of university theatre groups across the land. Shakespeare in performance is now reaching larger audiences than ever before in history. And as the BBC moves forward with plans to produce the entire Shakespeare canon over a period of six years—the most ambitious dramatic programming in the history of television—we can expect an even more powerful Shakespearean presence in the decade ahead.

"I am not only witty in myself," remarks Falstaff in a rare moment of self-analysis, "but the cause that wit is in other men." The same may be said of Falstaff's creator. Shakespeare's works more than those of any others (including Sir Walter Scott) have furnished librettos for grand opera. In his farmhouse villa outside Bussetto, a well-thumbed collected Shakespeare was Giuseppi Verdi's favorite book. Early in his career he made an opera of *Macbeth*, and near the end, when he was eighty, *The Merry Wives of Windsor* (and, to a lesser extent, *Henry IV*) furnished inspiration for his *Falstaff*. In between Verdi composed *Otello,* and at his death he left behind, in his own hand, a complete operatic libretto for *King Lear.* Choreographers have fashioned ballets from *A Midsummer Night's Dream, Othello,* and (more than once) *Romeo and Juliet.* On the musical stage *The Comedy of Errors* has metamorphosed into *The Boys from Syracuse*; transported to a Southern plantation, and equipped with a pulsating rock beat, *Othello* has become *Catch My Soul. The Taming of the Shrew* has inspired Cole Porter's wittiest score, that of *Kiss Me, Kate,* while the Montagues and Capulets, disguised as New York street gangs, have reenacted their timeless tragedy in an idiom as contemporary as Leonard Bernstein's *West Side Story.*

In the cinema Shakespeare has inspired notable film artists: Sir Laurence Olivier in England, Grigory Kozintsev in Russia, our own Orson Welles. Olivier's *Henry V* boosted homefront morale during dark days in World War II, and has uplifted innumerable spirits since. Birnam Wood—or its equivalent—marches shimmeringly across a Japanese landscape in *Throne of Blood,* Kurosawa's version of *Macbeth,* with the great Mifune as the tyrant dying in a hail of arrows. So, too, legitimate playwrights have nurtured their art with the Bard and put forth Shakespeare offshoots: Bertolt Brecht's *Coriolan,* Edward Bond's *Lear,* Peter Ustinov's *Romanoff and Juliet.* Shakespeare himself—and Tom Stoppard—to the contrary, Rosencrantz and Guildenstern are not dead.

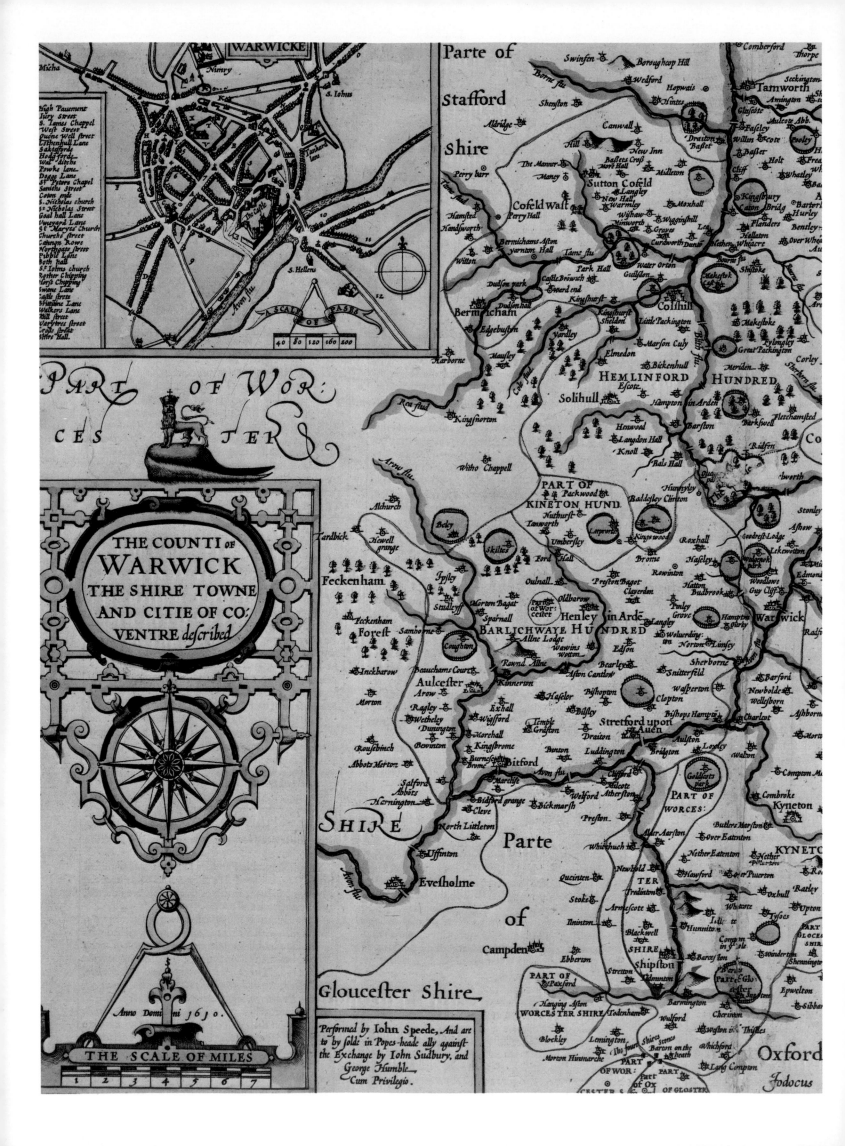

1

The Stratford Years

This royal throne of kings, this scept'red isle,
This earth of majesty, this seat of Mars,
This other Eden, demi-paradise,
This fortress built by Nature for herself
Against infection and the hand of war,
This happy breed of men, this little world,
This precious stone set in the silver sea,
Which serves it in the office of a wall,
Or as a moat defensive to a house,
Against the envy of less happier lands;
This blessed plot, this earth, this realm, this England....

Map of Warwickshire from John Speed's THEATRUM IMPERII MAGNAE BRITANNIAE (London, 1616). Shakespeare's Stratford-upon-Avon is located near the center of the lower half of the map.

This blessed plot, this earth, this realm, this England.... Thus in Shakespeare's *Tragedy of King Richard the Second* does the dying Gaunt apostrophize England in the accents of enraptured patriotism. Never mind that the play in which he figures dramatizes the inglorious reign, ending in deposition and regicide, of an irresponsible monarch; Richard's England was hardly a demi-paradise. Gaunt here speaks as "a prophet new inspir'd," reaching across the centuries to address a land whose potential for greatness had finally found fulfillment. That was the England of Elizabeth.

In April 1564, when Shakespeare was born, she had reigned for six years. Elizabeth's grandfather, the Earl of Richmond, had in 1485 defeated a superior army on a stretch of high ground overlooking Market Bosworth. Richmond's antagonist Richard III—Shakespeare's "poisonous bunchback'd toad"—had died fighting bravely in that encounter, and the victor was acclaimed on the battlefield as Henry VII, first in the Tudor line. In uniting the white rose of York with the red rose of Lancaster, Henry put an end to a long-drawn-out period of national decline—the loss of territories abroad, civil disorder, anarchy, and the emergence of a tyrant at home—and ushered in a new age. At least the new dynasty so interpreted the past. As an aspiring young dramatist a century later, Shakespeare would bring these tumultuous years to theatrical life in his first great historical tetralogy, the three parts of *Henry VI* followed by *Richard III*.

The first Tudor's son faced problems of a different sort. When Catherine of Aragon, his wife of many years, failed to produce a son to carry on the Tudor line, Henry VIII divorced her, an act that precipitated the Reformation in England. The monasteries were dissolved or seized, their wealth confiscated and their treasures pillaged. The decaying sanctuaries remained as mute reminders of past glories: in his 73rd Sonnet Shakespeare speaks of "Bare ruin'd choirs where late the sweet birds sang." Henry's second wife, Anne Boleyn, lasted three years before being executed. Rather than the son he coveted, she gave Henry a daughter, Elizabeth. He could not have guessed that she would become England's greatest monarch.

Anne Boleyn's successor, Jane Seymour, died in childbirth, but her sickly offspring survived. Henry had his son. Henry's fourth wife, Anne of Cleves, presented him with no children during their brief marriage of inconvenience, but she did give him a missal, inscribed "I beseech your Grace humble, when ye look on this, remember me. Your Grace's assured Anne, the daughter of Cleves." Assurance not having been made doubly sure, they soon parted. Two further marriages ensued

Opposite page, top: *Illuminated minia-ture of the Adoration of the Magi from ENCHIRIDION PRECLARE ECCLESIE SARISBURIENSIS (Paris, ca. 1533), a book of hours (containing prayers to be recited at the canonical hours, such as matins, nones, and vespers) present-ed by his fourth wife, Anne of Cleves, to Henry VIII. The inscription on the last leaf* (opposite page, bottom) *reads, in the original spelling: "I besiche your grace hūbl when ye loke on this remember me. yor gracis assured anne the dowgher off cleves."* This page, below: *the Presentation in the Temple, another miniature from the same Salisbury manual.*

before Henry, having become an unamiable monster, finally expired in 1547.

His son Edward reigned—without ruling—for six years and died before achieving his majority. Catholic Mary, daughter of Henry's first Queen, Catholic Catherine, followed. Within six months of her accession she had brought England back to Rome. Before her reign ended, Mary's pious zeal had created some three hundred Protestant martyrs. These victims of the Marian persecutions found their ideal hagiographer in John Foxe; his enormous *Acts and Monuments*, also known as *The Book of Martyrs*, was, with its numerous engraved illustrations, a book that had a profound impact on Shakespeare's age. The dramatist knew it, and turned to it as a source for Parts 2 and 3 of *Henry VI* and the episode of the conspiracy against Cranmer in *Henry VIII*.

Despite her efforts, Mary failed to reverse the tide of Reformation. In 1558 when she died, childless and pathologically dejected, the Established Church was re-established. The Elizabethan Age had arrived.

The land over which Elizabeth held sway was lovingly mapped out by Christopher Saxton, cartographer extraordinary. With probably only the most rudimentary instruments—a compass and measuring wheel, and maybe a plane-wheel such as explorers used—Saxton traveled high and low on horseback. To the mayors and justices he encountered he presented an official open letter, bidding them to see him "conducted unto any tower, castle, high place, or hill to view that country, and that he may be accompanied with two or three honest men such as do best know the country, for the better accomplishment of that service." Incredibly, Saxton required only six years to complete his appointed task of surveying and mapping the whole of England and Wales. In 1579 he published his atlas, consisting of a general map of England and thirty-four county maps. Oddly he depicted no roads, although these had existed in England since Roman times. But let that pass: Saxton's is the first national atlas ever produced anywhere,

and a masterpiece, artistic and cartographic, of the map-maker's art—a masterpiece, moreover, which, by demonstrating how engraved maps could be printed and marketed in large quantities, definitively established the enterprise in England. In the words of an eminent modern authority, "Saxton deserves a place beside Shakespeare as an interpreter of the national consciousness, unity and pride which were the greatest achievements of Elizabethan England." Poetry and drama were not the only good arts that thrived under the Virgin Queen. The interest taken by the Sovereign herself Saxton acknowledged by including the lion and dragon of the Tudor Royal Arms in each map.

Shakespeare hailed from Warwickshire, the vital midland of England. Taking its source from a spring called Avon Well in Northamptonshire, the River Avon flows westward across the breadth of the country: past hamlets and ruined abbeys; past fortressed Warwick, whose most celebrated earl went down in history as the Kingmaker (he figures in the *Henry VI* plays); past Charlecote, where Sir Thomas Lucy built the first Elizabethan mansion house in Warwickshire. Broadening, the swan-speckled river glides past Stratford-upon-Avon, the ancient market town with its collegiate church mirrored in the Avon's tranquil waters.

To the north, population growth had not yet wholly displaced the woodlands of Arden, with their wild deer and other game, their songbirds, and their many varieties of herbs and flowers. Shakespeare evokes this pastoral world in *As You Like It.* "They say he is already in the Forest of Arden," Charles reports of the old Duke, "and a many merry men with him; and there they live like the old Robin Hood of England. They say many young gentlemen flock to him every day, and fleet the time carelessly, as they did in the golden world." Technically, the golden world evoked in the play was situated in the Ardennes, on the border of Belgium and Luxembourg; but for Shakespeare (as for us) the Ardennes of his literary source and the Arden of his native Warwickshire became one beckoning wood.

John Foxe's ACTES AND MONUMENTS OF THESE LATTER AND PERILLOUS DAYES (London, 1563), also known as "The Book of Martyrs," was one of the most influential books of Elizabethan England and a powerful weapon of Protestant propaganda. The woodcut shown here depicts Thomas Cranmer, Archbishop of Canterbury, being burned at the stake in March 1556. Cranmer was one of 300 Protestants who suffered a fiery death during the reign of Queen Mary Tudor, whose zeal to re-establish Catholicism in England earned her the nickname "Bloody Mary."

Map of Warwickshire from the first English atlas, Christopher Saxton's ATLAS OF ENGLAND AND WALES (London, ca. 1579). Saxton, a young surveyor from Yorkshire working on the authority of Queen Elizabeth, completed thirty-five maps between 1574 and 1579, including a map of the county of Warwickshire locating Shakespeare's native town, Stratford-upon-Avon. Saxton's maps were decoratively embellished with engravings by Flemish and Dutch artists and hand-coloring by artisans employed by the publisher.

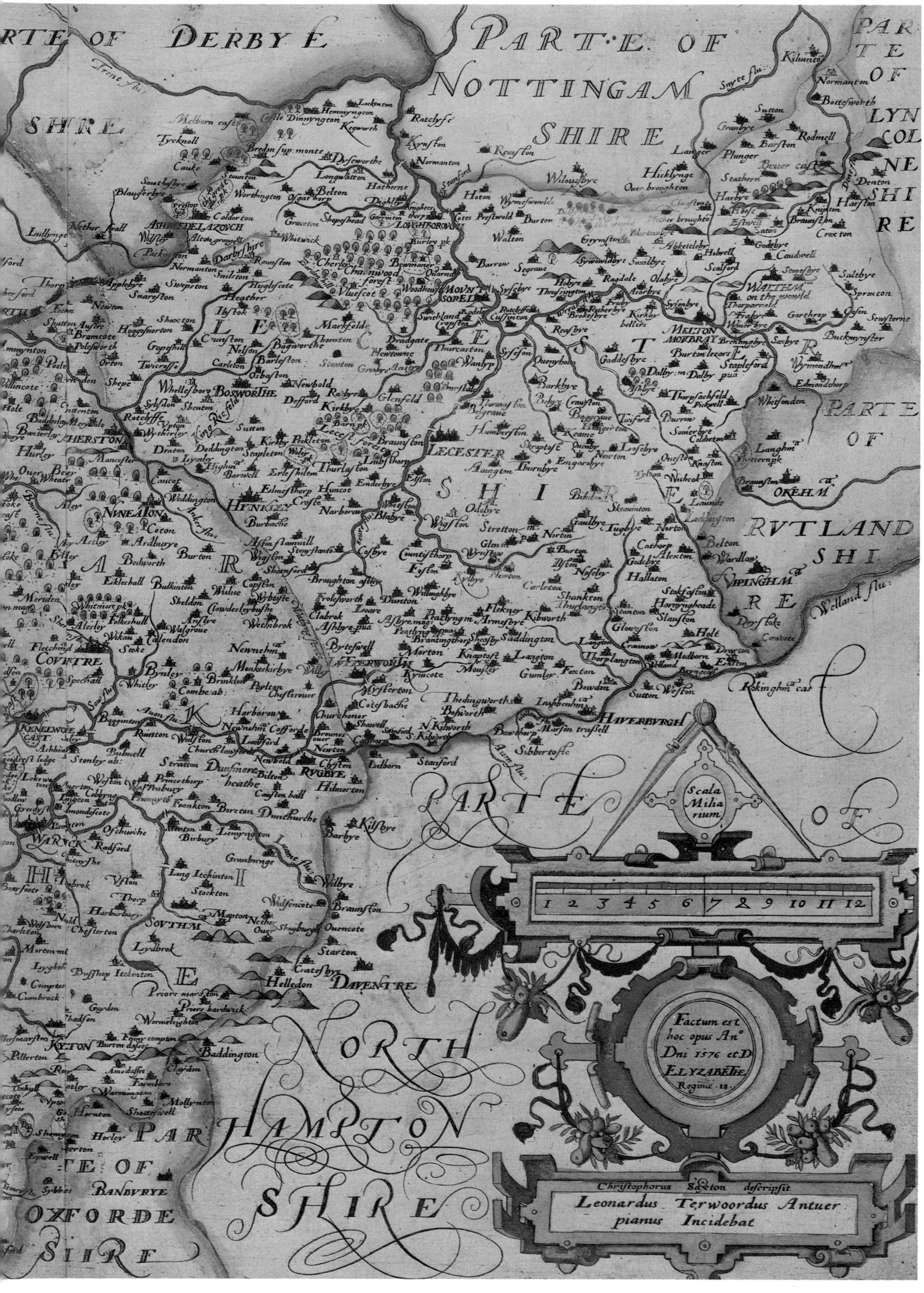

PARTE OF DERBYE

PARTE OF NOTTINGAM SHIRE

PARTE OF LYNCOLNE SHIRE

SHIRE

PARTE OF RVTLAND SHIRE

PARTE OF

LEICESTER SHIRE

WARR

COVETRE

KENELWOE CAST

WARWICK

PARTE OF BANBVRYE

OXFORDE SHIRE

NORTH HAMPTON SHIRE

PARTE OF

Scala Miliarium

1 2 3 4 5 6 7 8 9 10 11 12

Factum est hoc opus Anᵒ Dni 1576 et D. ELYZABETE Regine 18

Christophorus Saxton descripsit

Leonardus Terwoordus Antuerpianus Incidebat

NVNEATON
HYNKLEY
BOSWORTHE
ASHBIEDELAZOVCH
LOVGHBOROVGH
MOVNTSOREL
MELTON MOWBRAY
WALTHAM on the woulde
DAVENTRE
RVGBYE
SOVTHM
HAVERBVRGH
OKEHM
VPINGHM

*Map of England, from THEATRUM
IMPERII MAGNAE BRITANNIAE (London, 1616) by John Speed, the Latin
edition of an English atlas first published in 1612. Deriving from the work
of Christopher Saxton and other early
cartographers, Speed's atlas is more
elaborate than its predecessors, containing plans and views of English
towns as well as heraldic and other pictorial material. The border miniatures
show costumes of English citizens. The
two figures at left are a "Wilde Irish
Woman" (above) and a "Wilde Irish
Man" (below) from the border miniatures of Speed's map of Ireland in the
same volume.*

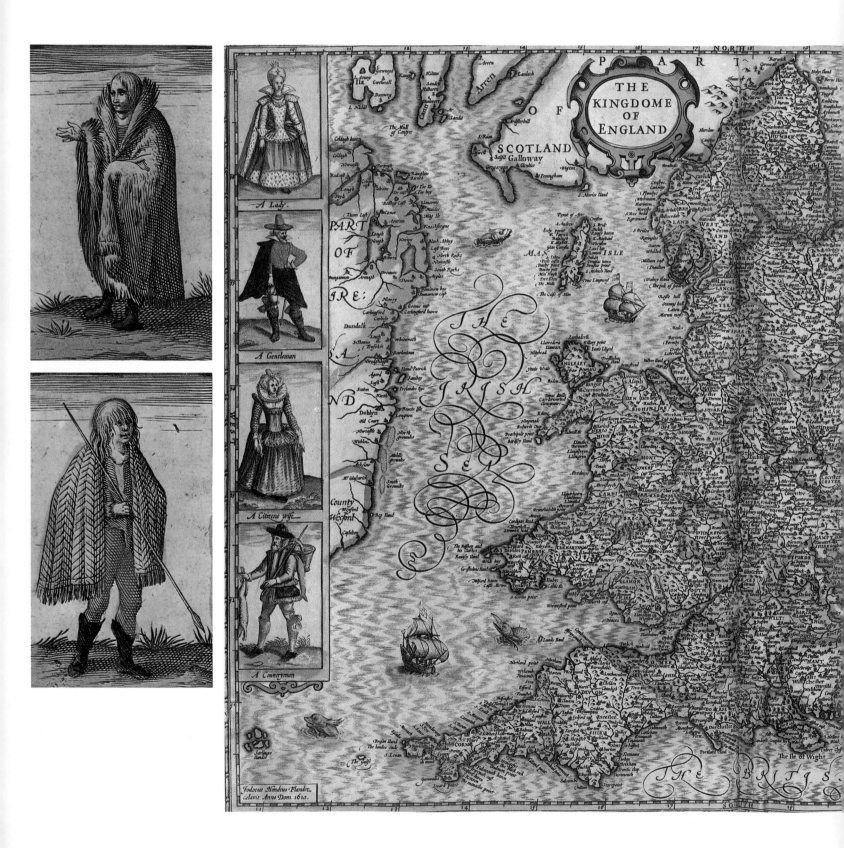

Another kind of domain lay to the south, the region known as the Feldon (that is, "fielden"): open country with ripe pasturage and broad fields. To the southwest, across from the Vale of the Red Horse and extending beyond to the counties of Worcestershire, Oxfordshire, Wiltshire, and Somersetshire, stretched the rolling Cotswold Hills. Here grazed the famous sheep, thick with fleece, that gave the hills their name. A later age would transform Birmingham, in the northwest corner of Warwickshire, into the industrial capital of the Midlands; in Shakespeare's day it was a small town whose streets resounded with the hammers and anvils of its smithies. Coventry, close by to Stratford, was already well developed as a clothmaking center especially noted for its cap-manufacture.

These and other townships, villages, streams, and landmarks Saxton denoted on his map of Warwickshire. As was his custom (followed by immediately succeeding cartographers), he used conventional trees for woodlands, and represented hills in shaded profile—a mode of depiction as ancient as Egyptian civilization. However impressive it was as an achievement, Saxton's atlas eventually gave way to others, of which the best known today is John Speed's *Theatre of the Empire of Great Britain,* published in 1611–12 and more than once reprinted. A prosperous Merchant Taylor, Speed gave his leisure hours to studying history, writing devotional tracts, and making maps. Although he cribbed from Saxton and John Norden, another great early cartographer, Speed cheerfully subscribed his work "Performed by John Speed." The arts cultivated by the Renaissance did not exclude the art of plagiarism. Speed enhanced the decorativeness and utility of his atlas, however, with various embellishments: inset plans of principal towns (Warwick and Coventry in his Warwickshire map); the arms of noble county families, such as the Earls of Warwick; and engravings illustrative of legendary and historical events (Edward IV, for example, being taken prisoner by his brother Clarence and Warwick at Wolney in 1469). In the larger general maps Speed included costume figures representative of the several estates: nobles, gentry, citizens, and country folk—even a wild Irish man and Irish woman. These hold a special interest for the social historian.

This page: *Plan of Stratford, ca. 1759, by Samuel Winter, the "writing master" in the local grammar school. This small ink and wash drawing, the earliest known plan of Stratford, was gathered into ARTISTIC RECORDS OF THE LIFE OF SHAKESPEARE by the ardent English Shakespearean and collector, James Orchard Halliwell-Phillipps, during the second half of the nineteenth century.*

Opposite page, top: *Shakespeare's Birthplace. An original watercolor by Phoebe Dighton (1834), later published in her RELICS OF SHAKESPEARE (Stratford-upon-Avon, 1835). This is one of the earliest published views of the house where Shakespeare was born.* Opposite page, bottom: *Stratford: church, river, and mill. Mid-nineteenth-century watercolor copy of an eighteenth-century painting.*

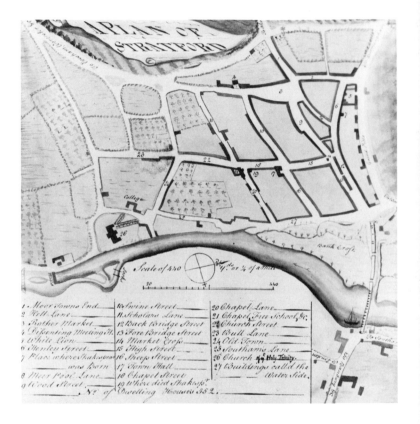

Not having yet become famous as the birthplace of William Shakespeare, Stratford failed to rate a place among Speed's inset maps. Nor has any plan of the town dating from Elizabethan times come down. A pity, but our sense of deprivation is mitigated by the fact that Stratford has not changed all that much over the centuries. The streets, broad and narrow because unconfined by any city wall, were laid out in the Middle Ages, the basic arrangement consisting of three thoroughfares parallel with the river, intersected by three others at right angles. That pattern has persisted to the present day. It can be seen in the earliest surviving plan, a watercolor made in the eighteenth century by Samuel Winter, a writing master in the local grammar school. Winter numbers and lists the streets and principal buildings, including (as item 7) the "Place where Shakespeare was Born" and (as 19) "Where died Shakespeare." In so doing he identifies the Birthplace in Henley Street, as well as New Place, for the first time.

John Shakespeare, the poet's father, was a householder in Henley Street some time before 1552, when he was fined (people in Stratford were always being fined) for making an unauthorized rubbish heap there. John had been reared in nearby Snitterfield, where his father and brother tilled the soil as tenant farmers. Stratford beckoned with broader horizons. There John became a successful glover and whittawer (or dresser of white and light-colored leather). He also received public recognition by holding various corporation offices, including, in 1568–69, that of bailiff: mayor, we would say. To his Henley Street house he brought his bride, Mary Arden, the youngest daughter of a well-to-do farmer in the district. The rambling two-story Arden farmhouse at Wilmcote, three miles from Stratford, still stands, visited by innumerable pilgrims as Mary Arden's House.

As John Shakespeare prospered, his family increased. A daughter, Joan, was baptized in 1558, and another daughter, Margaret, in 1562. In all, the Shakespeares, with the godparents, stood at the font eight times for the christening of four sons and four daughters. On April 26, 1564, the first-born son, William, was baptized. We do not know precisely when the poet was born—birth certificates as we know them did not yet exist—but traditionally Shakespeare's birth is celebrated on April 23rd, which conveniently happens also to be the day of St. George, England's patron saint. However that may be, on April 26th the vicar, John Bretchgirdle, followed the ceremony as set forth in *The Book of Common Prayer,* prescribing (after the reading of the Gospels and the minister's exhortation) that "Then the priest shall take the child in his hands, and ask the name, and naming the child, shall dip it in the water, so it be discreetly and warily done."

Below: *Holy Trinity Church, Stratford. Watercolor view from the southeast by J. C. Buckler (1823).*

Above: *THE CONTRACT AND TESTAMENT OF THE SOULE. Probably printed at St. Omer in France in 1638, this small devotional work was intended for use by English Catholics. "The Testament of the Soule" by Cardinal Borromeo, which forms the second part of the volume, is the only known printed version in English of a document discovered at Stratford in 1757 and since lost. That manuscript, known to scholars as "John Shakespeare's Spiritual Last Will and Testament," is sometimes interpreted as evidence that Shakespeare's father was a recusant— an Englishman who remained Catholic after Queen Elizabeth had created the "established" Church of England.*

Above: *The rite of infant baptism, a woodcut in A BOOKE OF CHRISTIAN PRAYERS (London, 1578), by Richard Day. This devotional manual is commonly known as "Queen Elizabeth's Prayer Book" because of the frontispiece showing the Queen at prayer. The decorative woodcut borders recall earlier Catholic prayer books.*

Below: *The order of baptism from the BOOKE OF COMMON PRAYER (London, 1594). The official book of the public worship of the Church of England was revised for the second time in 1559, early in Queen Elizabeth's reign, and went through more than one hundred printings before her death in 1603.*

Publique Baptiſme.

Then ſhall the Prieſt ſay.

Eing nolve dearly belooued brethren, that theſe children be regenerate and grafted into the bodie of Chriſtes Congregation, let vs giue thanks vnto God for theſe benefites, and with one accorde make our prayers vnto Almightie God, that they may leade the reſt of their life according to this beginning.

Elizabeth's Prayer Book provided for the administration of the sacraments, rites, and ceremonies of the Church of England. As its most recent editor puts it, *The Book of Common Prayer* furnished "the context in which Elizabethans, from Queen Elizabeth and William Shakespeare to the village housewife and yeoman farmer, lived and died." The first Prayer Book had appeared in 1549, in the reign of Edward VI. A second, more clearly Protestant in emphasis, followed three years later, but was repealed in Mary's time—"to the great decay," as Elizabeth's Parliament declared, "of the due honor of God and discomfort to the professors of the truth of Christ's religion." When Elizabeth became Queen, an Act of Supremacy restored to the Crown the authority over the Church that Henry VIII had held, while an Act of Uniformity reintroduced the Prayer Book in a revised form. The third edition of 1559 was the one by which all Elizabethans worshiped. And all law-abiding Elizabethans, men and women, *did* worship, for the statutes of the realm required them to attend their parish church each Sunday. The Prayer Book specified the proper lessons to be read at matins and evensong throughout the year, either from the Great Bible or from the Bishops' Bible or the Geneva Bible: the versions of Scripture then readily accessible. After a century of religious turmoil, the Elizabethan Settlement—a *via media* between Rome and Geneva—had established a precarious equilibrium that would last until the Puritan revolution of the next age.

Shakespeare would have received his earliest religious indoctrination not at Holy Trinity Church but in his parents' house. Many in this period, despite their outward conformity, held to the Old Faith. Recusants, as they were called, were numerous in Stratford and environs. The particular form of belief to which the Shakespeares subscribed has been much debated, with no conclusive answers forthcoming. In the eighteenth century a spiritual last will and testament—a Catholic profession of faith—surfaced in the Birthplace rooftiles. Reportedly it bore the name of John Shakespeare, but the document has since disappeared, and most authorities remain skeptical. Nevertheless, such testaments, composed by Carlo Borromeo, the Cardinal Archbishop of Milan, did exist, and were circulated in England as well as on the Continent as an instrument of Counter-Reformation.

Whatever their beliefs, the Shakespeares are unlikely to have read the Bible aloud to their children at the family hearth, for they were apparently illiterate. Mary witnessed legal documents with her mark, a cross; so did her husband, although he also used as his sign manual a pair of compasses emblematic of his glover's trade. In this respect he was like most others of his class, and in any event he came from a village that had no school. Stratford was more fortunate. There the King's New School offered pupils the rigorous curriculum of the Elizabethan grammar school. For John Shakespeare's sons tuition was free—a lucky circumstance, for he fell on hard times while William was growing up.

Not surprisingly, pupil rosters and the like from Shakespeare's day have failed to come down, but it is a reasonable inference, supported by the body of his works, that he did indeed receive a grammar-school education in the only institution available for that purpose in Stratford. The school stood but five minutes' walk from the family domicile in Henley Street. Shakespeare's education, begun at the age of four or five, would for the first couple of years have taken place at the attached petty school. There, under the supervision of the usher (the master's assistant), William would have learned the alphabet and elements of syllabication from the hornbook, which also included, for his improvement, the Lord's Prayer. A hornbook consisted of a single printed leaf, overlaid with thin transparent horn and framed in wood. Having mastered what it offered, the young scholars proceeded to the *ABC with the Catechism* (which provided figures), and then to *The Primer and Catechism,* containing the seven penitential psalms and other devotional matter, as well as the Calendar and Almanac. The catechism, first promulgated in 1549, instilled obedience, respect for authority, and Christian love: "My duty towards my neighbor is to love him as myself, and to do to all men as I would they should do unto me; to love, honor, and succor my father and mother; to submit myself to all my governors, teachers, spiritual pastors, and masters; to order myself lowly and reverently to all my betters...."

Next came the grammar school proper, where William Lily's *Short Introduction of Grammar*—a standard textbook—initiated the pupils into the mysteries of grammar: Latin grammar, as prescribed by the Humanist educational theorists. However Shakespeare felt about this regimen at the time (and one can guess), he evidently remembered his lessons well enough, for he lifted a passage from Lily for the scene in *The Merry Wives of Windsor* where Sir Hugh Evans, the parson-pedagogue, puts little Master William through his paces in the presence of the lad's disgruntled mother and Mistress Quickly:

> *Evans.* Come hither, William; hold up your head; come.
> *Mrs. Page.* Come on, sirrah; hold up your head; answer your master; be not afraid.
> . . . . . .
> *Evans....* What is 'fair,' William?
> *William.* Pulcher.
> *Quickly.* Polecats! There are fairer things than polecats, sure.
> *Evans.* You are a very simplicity 'oman; I pray you, peace. What is 'lapis,' William?
> *William.* A stone.
> *Evans.* And what is 'a stone,' William?
> *William.* A pebble.
> *Evans.* No, it is 'lapis'; I pray you remember in your prain.

CATECHISMVS

paruus pueris primùm Latinè qui ediscatur, proponendus in Scholis.

✠ A a b c d e f g h i k l m n o p q
r ſ s t u v w x y z.　　ã ẽ ĩ õ ũ:
A B C D E F G H I K L M N O
P Q R S T U W X Y Z.

a e i o u	a e i o u
ab eb ib ob ub	ba be bi bo bu
ac ec ic oc uc	ca ce ci co cu
ad ed id od ud	da de di do du

In the name of the Father, and of
the ſon, & of the holy Ghoſt. Amen.

Ur father which art in heauen, hallowed be thy name.
Thy kingdome come. Thy
will bee done in earth as it is in
heauen. Giue vs this day our daily
bread. And forgiue vs our treſpaſ-
ſes, as wee forgiue them that treſ-
pas againſt vs, and lead vs not into temptation. But deliuer vs
from euill. Amen.

Opposite page: *Hornbook dating from Shakespeare's lifetime. Young William probably learned his ABCs from a hand-held hornbook such as this. Paper printed in black letter (or gothic) type was mounted on wood and overlaid by a protective sheet of transparent animal horn.*

Below: *The Latin title page to part two of this copy of William Lily's SHORT INTRODUCTION OF GRAMMAR (Geneva, 1557) shows the scribbles of an early owner. Since schoolbooks received hard use, few copies of this standard textbook have survived.*

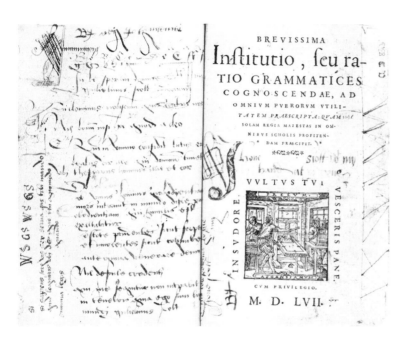

Thus trained in their grammar, the scholars went on, in succeeding forms, to the literary and rhetorical classics, as well as to history—Roman history, it goes without saying. The comedies of Plautus would have introduced Shakespeare to the five-act structure of plays. But Ovid, especially *The Metamorphoses,* would remain Shakespeare's favorite classical poet, to be drawn upon over and over again. In *The Tempest,* a very late play, Prospero's magical speech renouncing his magic—

> I'll break my staff,
> Bury it certain fathoms in the earth,
> And deeper than did ever plummet sound
> I'll drown my book.

—draws upon Medea's incantation (*Metamorphoses,* vii.197–209), which Shakespeare consulted both in the original Latin and in Arthur Golding's popular translation. In his great encomium Ben Jonson speaks of Shakespeare's "small Latin and less Greek." Small Latin, perhaps, by Jonson's yardstick, but not by ours. As for the Greek, Shakespeare would acquire his smattering in the Upper School, using the Greek New Testament for constructions.

The Elizabethan school day was unmercifully long, running from six or seven in the morning until five or six in the afternoon, every day but Sunday. In the "sweet o' the year," especially, "When proud-pied April, dress'd in all his trim, / Hath put a spirit of youth in every thing," the young Shakespeare must have turned whenever possible to another book, more congenial to the schoolboy spirit. This was the book of nature, open to him in the gardens, orchards, and hedgerows of leafy Stratford, along the Avon's banks, and in the beckoning fields and woodlands just outside.

"Flowers I noted," the poet says in Sonnet 99, and in fourteen brief lines the forward violet, the lily, the buds of marjoram, and the roses standing fearfully on thorns all find their place. Shakespeare's works comprise a brilliantly colored garden in which flowers, wild and cultivated, flourish side by side. Violets spring everywhere. They "strew the green lap of the new come spring." Their scent (in *Hamlet*) is said to be "sweet not lasting, / The perfume and suppliance of a minute; / No more." Transiently expressive of life, violets flourish amid the dead laid to rest in country churchyards: "Lay her i' th' earth," Laertes cries over Ophelia's coffin, "And from her fair and unpolluted flesh / May violets spring!" As botanists have observed, the violet grows with the flower inverted, to prevent rain damage to the pollen. Shakespeare may not have known this scientific explanation, but he observed the posture of "the nodding violet" in *A Midsummer Night's Dream.*

Other flowers in the Shakespeare garden include "pale primroses" ("That die unmarried ere they can behold /Bright Phoebus in his strength"), pansies (the "little western flower" maidens call "Love-in-idleness"), daffodils, narcissuses, freckled cowslips, daisies pied, silver-white lady-smocks, and many more besides. Above all, the roses bloom: white, red, variegated, musk, and damask. Eight varieties are cited altogether, while the word *rose,* or *roses,* appears over one hundred times. As in all gardens, cankers threaten the buds, and caterpillars nibble away the leaves. Fast-growing weeds—darnel, nettle, rank fumiter, thistle, dock, and spear-grass—will, if suffered, "o'ergrow the garden / And choke the herbs for want of husbandry." Among Shakespeare's herbs are thyme, rue, savory, parsley, and rosemary ("There's rosemary, that's for remembrance").

Along the river's bank the young Shakespeare would have noticed sedge, rushes (used to strew the floors of Tudor houses), and the tall reeds which thatched the roofs of humble cottages. "His tears," Ariel says of the good Lord Gonzalo in *The Tempest,* "run down his beard, like winter's drops / From eaves of reeds." In the stream the green leaves of the vagabond flags would have swayed to and fro in "the varying tide," while the willow trees growing along the water's edge—"The rank of osiers by the murmuring stream" (*As You Like It*)—would have cast their gray reflection. Traditionally the willow symbolized forsaken love. Desdemona sings a song of willow before she dies. And in perhaps the most famous floral passage in Shakespeare, the willow frames the scene of Ophelia's drowning as described by Queen Gertrude:

> There is a willow grows aslant the brook
> That shows his hoar leaves in the glassy stream;
> Therewith fantastic garlands did she make
> Of crowflowers, nettles, daisies, and long purples
> That liberal shepherds give a grosser name,
> But our cold maids do dead men's fingers call them.
> There, on the pendent boughs her coronet weeds
> Clamb'ring to hang, an envious sliver broke;
> When down her weedy trophies and herself
> Fell in the weeping brook.

If Shakespeare's works are a scented garden that invite the horticulturist's interest, they hold too the pleasures of the arboretum. Warwickshire offered a variety of trees and shrubs. Blight had not yet reduced the elms, of which, in Stratford town, almost a thousand shaded corporation property, according to a survey made in 1582. But curiously, Shakespeare names elms only three times. Among the other trees he mentions are the pine, box, ash, oak, and aspen. Shrubs and vines include gorse, bramble, ivy, dewberry,

A variety of plants from the finely illustrated botanical book, or herbal, DEN NIEUWEN HERBARIUS (Basel, 1550) by Leonhard Fuchs, a German botanist after whom the fuchsia was named. Among the plants depicted are the hollyhock, rosemary, rose, violet, lily, and members of the melon family. Somewhat rarer than the original Latin edition published one year earlier, this Dutch translation of "The New Herbal" was hand-painted by the publisher's colorists.

hyssop (used for medicinal tea and syrup), and hawthorne. Some trees have traditional associations. The witches in *Macbeth* find room in their broth for slips of yew "Sliver'd in the moon's eclipse"; dismal yews also grow among the gravestones in Verona's cemetery in *Romeo and Juliet*. Similarly ill-omened is the elder tree, from which (it is said) Judas hanged himself; an elder fittingly overshades the infernal forest pit in *Titus Andronicus*. The oak, although vulnerable to lightning, betokens strength; Coriolanus, in the Watch's words, is "the rock, the oak not to be wind-shaken." In all, Shakespeare's plant inventory comprises over 150 varieties, according to one tabulation.

Bird references, while less numerous, occur often enough to keep a drowsy ornithologist awake. Shakespeare's birds range from the lark, herald of the morn, to the nightingale, Philomel, that sweet night singer. They include birds of prey and carrion—the eagle, kite, raven, vulture, and owl—as well as game birds (woodcock, partridge), water fowl (swans, wild geese, loons, dive-dappers, and mallard), and familiar songbirds (the blackbird, redbreast, and throstle or thrush). For his bird-lore, as has been often noted, Shakespeare draws upon inherited typologies. The phoenix rises from its ashes, the pelican feeds her young with her own blood. The blackness of the raven and the whiteness of the dove retain their time-honored associations. Shrieking night-owls bode ill, especially at a birth, as Richard III's example demonstrates. Fools are called gulls or choughs. But observation rather than lore lies behind Puck's simile in *A Midsummer Night's Dream:*

> As wild geese that the creeping fowler eye,
> Or russet-pated choughs, many in sort,
> Rising and cawing at the gun's report.

So also with Banquo's lines, unexpected and strangely evocative, as Duncan's party beholds Macbeth's castle at Dunsinane:

> This guest of summer,
> The temple-haunting martlet, does approve
> By his lov'd mansionry that the heaven's breath
> Smells wooingly here; no jutty, frieze,
> Buttress, nor coign of vantage, but this bird
> Hath made his pendent bed and procreant cradle.
> Where they most breed and haunt, I have observ'd
> The air is delicate.

Along with plants and birds, beasts and insects. Some of these creatures the young Shakespeare would have encountered on, or near, his Warwickshire doorstep: the harmless necessary cat, the farmer's dog barking at the beggar, the "breeding jennet, lusty, young, and proud," that "rushes, snorts, and neighs aloud." In *Antony and Cleopatra* the inexpressibly charismatic Serpent of old Nile hoists sail and

flees like a cow in June, the breese—stinging flies—upon her. On neighboring farms, such as the one his Uncle Henry worked in Snitterfield, Shakespeare would have seen the livestock with their offspring. Making his way from Henley Street to the Avon, he would have passed the shambles in Middle Row and there become acquainted with death as a fact of rural life. Later, in *2 Henry VI*, the abattoir would provide the simile for good Duke Humphrey as the threatened calf:

> And as the butcher takes away the calf,
> And binds the wretch, and beats it when it strays,
> Bearing it to the bloody slaughter-house,
> Even so, remorseless, have they borne him hence;
> And as the dam runs lowing up and down,
> Looking the way her harmless young one went,
> And can do naught but wail her darling's loss. . . .

In the fragrant fields, on the hills with their sheep flocks, and in woodland clearings, Shakespeare would have heard the cry of hounds and the winding of the hunter's horn as men on horseback pursued other fearful creatures: the timorous fleeting hare, the subtle fox, the roe "which no encounter dare." A deer hunt fills the whole second act of *Titus Andronicus* and assumes the dimensions of metaphor, as Lavinia becomes the dainty doe brutally brought to earth by her rapists. Smaller living things—vermin, burrowing creatures, and the like—also find their place in the Shakespearean scheme. These include the blind mole and the hedgehog, the fretful porpentine with its quills on end, the weasel purloining eggs from unguarded nests. Even the humble snail, with its tender horn, does not escape the poet's sympathetic eye. Insects buzz and sting. Gnats dance in the sun. Bees have waxen thighs. The glow-worm "shows the matin to be near" by beginning "to pale his uneffectual fire" (a trifling mistake, by the way, for it is the female, not the male, of the species which glows).

Bears, such as the unfriendly fellow that pursues Antigonus to his eternal exit in *The Winter's Tale*, Shakespeare would more likely have observed in the animal-baiting arenas of his London theatre-land than in tamer Warwickshire. The lioness "with udders all drawn dry," crouching with catlike watch under the bush's shade in *As You Like It*, was no more native to the Ardennes than to Arden. She belongs with the more exotic members of the Shakespeare bestiary—with the elephant (with joints, "but none for courtesy"), with camels, leopards, and the unicorn, with "the rugged Russian bear, / The arm'd rhinoceros, or th' Hyrcan tiger." But these are merely alluded to, the unicorn (in *The Tempest*) skeptically. On the other hand, poor Wat, the relentlessly hunted hare in *Venus and Adonis*, is part of a real vernal world fondly

Left: *A hand-colored woodcut of a fallow deer from Edward Topsell's HISTORIE OF FOURE-FOOTED BEASTES (London, 1607) Topsell, an English clergyman, based his text and illustrations largely on the work of the German naturalist Konrad Gesner, who lived a half-century earlier.*
Right: *The owl, the duck, and the stork as depicted in an early ornithology, Pierre Belon's L'HISTOIRE DE LA NATURE DES OYSEAUX (Paris, 1555), a French naturalist's early attempt at bird classification.*

Opposite page: *Country games, as depicted in the crude woodcut frontispiece to* ANNALIA DUBRENSIA *(London, 1636), printed for Matthew Walbanke. The book contains poems celebrating the annual Cotswold Games, popular in Shakespeare's time.*

evoked. Outrunning the wind, turning and crossing, bounding through gaps in hedges and fences, he reaches the illusory safety of the hilltop:

> By this, poor Wat, far off upon a hill,
> Stands on his hinder legs with list'ning ear,
> To hearken if his foes pursue him still;
> Anon their loud alarums he doth hear;
>   And now his grief may be compared well
>   To one sore sick that hears the passing-bell.
>
> Then shalt thou see the dew-bedabbled wretch
> Turn and return, indenting with the way;
> Each envious briar his weary legs do scratch,
> Each shadow makes him stop, each murmur stay;
>   For misery is trodden on by many,
>   And being low never reliev'd by any.

It is Venus who speaks these lines, and with an ulterior purpose—she would dissuade her beloved Adonis from the dangers of the boar hunt—but who would question that the poet numbered poor Wat among his familiar acquaintances?

Such sympathies notwithstanding, Shakespeare may well have hunted. Certainly other high-spirited youth of Warwickshire did so, and the plays and poems yield a sufficiency of knowledgeable allusion. Dr. Johnson had a point (as usual) when he observed, "He that will understand Shakespeare, must not be content to study him in the closet, he must look for his meaning sometimes among the sports of the field...." Possibly now and then Shakespeare did some poaching, the offense of venery being in those days reckoned venial. A legend originating in the aftermath of Shakespeare's death has him poaching deer on the grounds of Charlecote, Sir Thomas Lucy's estate four miles upstream from Stratford. Later scholarship has shown that Charlecote did not then have a legally empaled park for beasts of chase, such as the fallow deer, but instead a free-warren stocked with rabbits, pheasants, wood pigeons, and similar small game. Still, roe deer, only slightly less tempting to the sportsman, might have roamed at Charlecote in Shakespeare's day. The legend, which has come down from several sources, possibly has some basis in fact.

The countryside also offered opportunities for bird-snaring (with lime, traps, or nets), fishing, archery, falconry, and coursing; chances also, in Samuel Rowlands's indefatigable enumeration in *The Letting of Humours' Blood in the Head-Vein,*

> To jump or leap over ditch or hedge;
> To wrestle, play at stool-ball, or to run,
> To pitch the bar, or to shoot off a gun;
> To play at loggets, nineholes, or ten pins,
> To try it out at football, by the shins;

> At tick-tack, Irish, noddy, maw, and ruff,
> At hot cockles, leap-frog, or blind-man buff....

Multitudes gathered each year at Whitsuntide to take part in the Elizabethan country Olympics celebrated in the Cotswold Hills. The Cotswold Games go back at least to the last quarter of the sixteenth century—maybe earlier. When James ascended the throne in 1603, he appointed Robert Dover, an attorney from Barton-on-the-Heath in the Shakespeare country, to manage the games. Resettled in the Cotswold village of Stanway, Captain Dover (as he was called) presided, splendidly attired in his monarch's cast-off finery. Thousands competed on the green, running, leaping, throwing the bar, wrestling, and hunting, while the local nymphs danced for prizes; so an enthusiast rhapsodizes in *Annalia Dubrensia*. In a panegyric to Dover in the same volume, Thomas Heywood, Shakespeare's fellow dramatist, compares him with Hercules:

> There is an equal balance in your fames,
> He made the Olympic, thou the Cotswold games,
> And who can say is best? Not I, nor he;
> Of him we have only heard, but we know thee.
> Thee (noble Dover) then go on; be still
> The man thou art, and maintain Cotswold Hill.
>   So when thy glass is run and sand is past.
>   Thy name and fame shall Hercules outlast.

Whether Dover's fame outlasted Hercules' is perhaps doubtful, but he did superintend the Cotswold Games for forty years.

According to Caroline Spurgeon, who laboriously tabulated and classified Shakespeare's images, the dramatist had no real knowledge of, or interest in, fishing. Swimming was something else, and surely the description of Ferdinand's escape after shipwreck in *The Tempest* has an assurance compatible with the actual experience of swimming. "I saw him beat the surges under him," Francisco reports,

> And ride upon their backs; he trod the water,
> Whose enmity he flung aside, and breasted
> The surge most swoln that met him; his bold head
> 'Bove the contentious waves he kept, and oared
> Himself with his good arms in lusty stroke
> To th' shore, that o'er his wave-worn basis bowed,
> As stooping to relieve him.

On the basis of impressions drawn from Shakespeare's imagery, Spurgeon arrives at a picture of the poet as a physical being. "The figure of Shakespeare which emerges," she finds, "is of a compactly well-built man, probably on the slight side, extraordinarily well co-ordinated, lithe and nimble of body, quick and accurate of eye, delighting in swift muscular movement." Even if one questions whether literary evidence

COTSWOLD GAMES.

ANNALIA DVBRENSIA.

Vpon the yeerely celebration of M.ʳ ROBERT DOVERS Olimpick Games vpon *Cotswold-Hills.*

Written by

MICHAELL DRAYTON. Esq.	IOHN TRVSSELL. Gent.
IOHN TRVSSELL. Gent.	WILLIAM COLE. Gent.
WILLIAM DVRHAM. Oxon,	FERRIMAN.RVTTER. Oxon.
WILLIAM DENNY. Esq.	IOHN STRATFORD. Gent.
THOMAS RANDALL. Gent.	THOMAS SANFORD. Gent.
BEN: IOHNSON.	ROBERT GRIFFIN. Gent.
IOHN DOVER. Gent.	IOHN COLE. Gent.
OWEN FELTHAM. Gent.	ROBERT DVRHAM. Oxon.
FRANCIS IZOD. Gent.	A SIRINX Oxon.
NICHOLAS WALLINGTON. Ox.	IOHN MONSON. Esq.
IOHN BALLARD. Oxon.	WALTON POOLE. Gent.
TIMOTHY OGLE. Gent.	RICHARD WELLS. Oxon.
WILLIAM AMBROSE. Oxon.	WILLIAM FORTH. Esq.
WILLIAM BELLAS. Gent.	SHACK: MARMYON. Gent.
THOMAS COLE. Oxon.	R N.
WILLIAM BASSE. Gent.	THOMAS HEYWOOD. Gent.
CAPTAINE MENESE.	

LONDON,
Printed by *Robert Raworth,* for *Mathewe Walbancke.* 1636.

of the sort on which Spurgeon depends can properly be used for such purposes, she may well be right. John Aubrey, still in touch with a living tradition, records in his "Brief Life" of Shakespeare that "he was a handsome, well-shaped man," and we have no reason to believe otherwise.

However lithe and well-shaped he grew up to be, he necessarily spent much of his time indoors as a boy. In winter, with its inclemencies and short days, school was perhaps more tolerable. This was the season, as the song holds at the end of *Love's Labor's Lost:*

> When icicles hang by the wall,
> And Dick the shepherd blows his nail,
> And Tom bears logs into the hall,
> And milk comes frozen home in pail,
> When blood is nipp'd, and ways be foul,
> Then nightly sings the staring owl:
> 'Tu-who;
> To-whit, Tu-who'—A merry note,
> While greasy Joan doth keel the pot.

Pastimes moved indoors, beside the hearth. Many of these, venerable in Shakespeare's day, have currency yet in our own, though sometimes in modified form. Needle work was as popular then as now. People diced and played cards despite Puritan denunciations of these inventions of the devil.

A Booke of fishing with Hooke & Line, and of all other instruments there-unto belonging.

Another of sundrie Engines and Trappes to take Polcats, Buzards, Rattes, Mice and all other kindes of Vermine & Beasts whatsoever, most profitable for all Warriners, and such as delight in this kinde of sport and pastime.

Made by L. M.

DONDON.
Printed by Iohn Wolfo, and are to be solde by Edwarde White dwelling at the little North doore of Paules at the signe of the Gunne.
1 5 9 9.

Left: *The country pastimes of fishing and trapping are discussed in Leonard Mascall's BOOKE OF FISHING WITH HOOKE & LINE... ANOTHER OF SUNDRIE ENGINES AND TRAPPES TO TAKE POLCATS, BUZARDS, RATTES, MICE AND ALL OTHER KINDES OF VERMINE & BEASTS (London, 1590). The author was a clerk of the kitchen to Matthew Parker, Archbishop of Canterbury.*

Center: *Two of the traps depicted by Mascall, a latch-trap (above) and a foot-trap (below) for catching foxes.* Right: *Everard Digby's DE ARTE NATANDI (London, 1587) was the earliest manual published in England on the art of swimming. The woodcut illustrations depict the joys of plunging naked into a country stream, and the instruction is presented in the form of a dialogue between teacher (Geronicus) and pupil (Neugenes).*

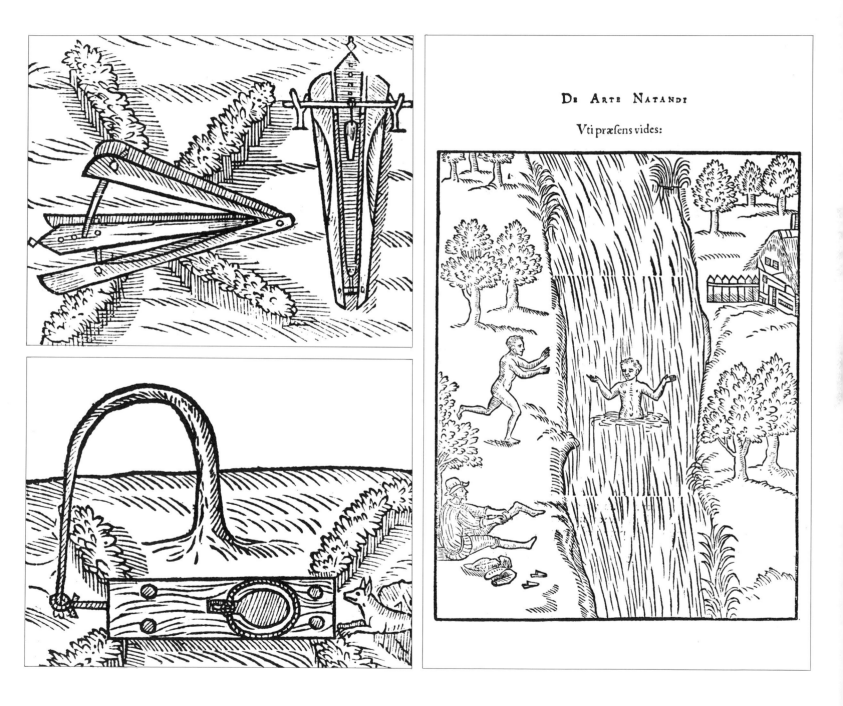

Our phrase "main chance" comes from hazard, the dice game in which the caster called a "main"—any number from five to nine—before throwing. Hazard provides the imagery for Hotspur contemplating the risks of battle in *1 Henry IV:*

> Were it good
> To set the exact wealth of all our states
> All at one cast? To set so rich a main
> On the nice hazard of one doubtful hour?

The expression "main chance" itself occurs only twice in Shakespeare: Warwick, in *2 Henry IV,* remarks on men's power to prophesy "of the main chance of things / As yet not come to life." Of card games, primero, maw (also known as Five Cards), trump (a forerunner of whist), noddy, and gleek were among the many popular variations.

Young and old enjoyed backgammon, then called Tables, while the more philosophical preferred chess. At the denouement of *The Tempest* Shakespeare achieves a striking effect by having Prospero "discover" the young lovers playing chess:

> *Miranda.* Sweet lord, you play me false.
> *Ferdinand.*   No, my dearest love,
>   I would not for the world.
> *Miranda.* Yes, for a score of kingdoms you should wrangle,
>   And I would call it fair play.

Of Shakespeare's contemporaries Thomas Middleton especially exploited the dramatic possibilities of chess. Chess is richly mined for *double entendre* in the seduction scene of his *Women Beware Women;* and the game furnishes the guiding stage metaphor for his sensationally successful topical play, *A Game at Chess.*

Chess and dice and cards were occupations for idle hours. Meanwhile, indoors and out, the domestic round went on: bread was baked, pots were scrubbed.

> He kills his swine and minds to make good cheer,
> To pass the time while winter's rage doth cease.

Thus does Thomas Fella apostrophize the "careful man" when he comes to December in the calendar for his commonplace *Book of Divers Devices.* The delightfully primitive accompanying illustration shows a porker contentedly boiling in his pot.

Entertainment of another kind, more sophisticated and more fatefully relevant to Shakespeare's later career, came to Stratford when the actors, in much the same fashion as the players at Hamlet's Elsinore, included the town in their wanderings. The first professional troupe to visit Stratford was the Queen's Men. They arrived in 1569, when John Shakespeare was bailiff. Did little William, then five, sit restlessly beside his father in the Guild Hall when they

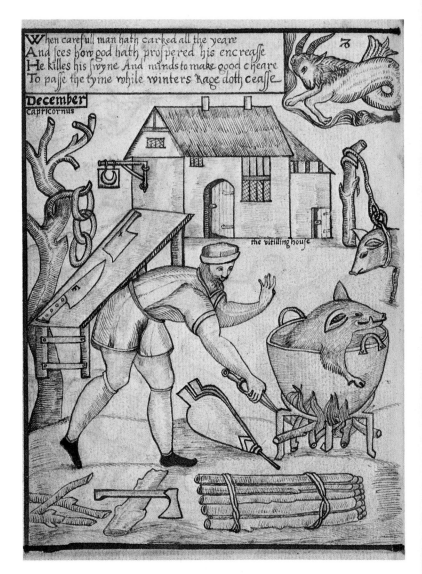

Left: *Country occupations for the month of December are depicted in this ink drawing from Thomas Fella's commonplace book, A BOOKE OF DIVEIRS DEVISES, completed between 1585 and 1622. Normally, a commonplace book was a manuscript in which the owner recorded quotations or other material worthy of remembrance. Pictorial commonplace books such as this are unusual. The author, not a professional artist or scrivener, was identified in* 1964 as a cloth merchant of Halesworth in Suffolk. He made this book of 162 drawings for his own entertainment, but it offers later generations vivid glimpses of sixteenth-century English life.

Center: *A crewel embroidery pattern from the time of Shakespeare in Thomas Trevelyon's PICTORIAL COMMONPLACE BOOK of 1608.*

Right: *A treatise on chess, THE MOST ANCIENT AND LEARNED PLAYE, CALLED THE PHILOSOPHERS GAME (London, 1563), variously attributed to Ralph Lever and William Fulwood, whose initials appear on the title page. This, the only known surviving copy of the first edition, is bound with another early treatise on chess, THE PLEASAUNT AND WITTIE PLAYE OF THE CHEASTS RENEWED (1562), translated from the Italian of Damiano da Odemira.*

Right, bottom: *Title page of Thomas*

This page: Staging diagram for THE CASTLE OF PERSEVERANCE, the oldest extant Morality Play, the earliest known (dating from the vast English (Unlike the vast ... 1425). Unlike the vast ... which dramatized ... Moralities pers... as Mankind ... The uni... from ... T...

THE MOST ANCIENT
and learned playe, called the Philosophers game, inuented for the honest recreation of students, and other sober persons, in passing the tediousnes of tyme, to the release of their labours, and the exercise of their wittes.
Set forth with such playne precepts, rules, and tables, that all men with ease may understand it, and most men with pleasure practise it. By W. F.

Printed at London by Rouland Hall, for Iames Roubothum, the yere 1563. the 21. of May.

A Gam at Chæss as it was Acted nine days together at the Globe

...e earli-
...ay in
...period 1400–
...Mystery cycles,
...Biblical events,
...nified abstractions such
...and the Seven Deadly Sins.
...ue Folger manuscript (dating
...ca. 1440) containing THE CAS-
...E OF PERSEVERANCE and two other
Morality Plays was once owned by the
Reverend Cox Macro (1683–1767), and
these three late-medieval didactic enter-
tainments are therefore known as the
Macro Plays.

Opposite Page: *Original watercolor of
the Last Judgment, showing Hell-mouth
(a subject frequently depicted in early
Mystery Plays) in the lower right corner.
This is one of a series of paintings on
the wall of the Stratford Guild Chapel,
which had been white-washed to
remove Catholic imagery while Shakespeare's father was one of the town officials. Rediscovered in 1804, the wall
paintings were carefully copied by
Thomas Fisher, who published them in
1807.*

performed? Other companies followed—Leicester's Men, led
by James Burbage, in 1573, Warwick's, Strange's, Derby's, and
others afterwards. No fewer than seven different companies
acted in the Guild Hall between 1579 and 1584. This despite
the fact that the theatrical industry, as such, was then new to
England. When Shakespeare was born, a structure purpose-
built for the representation of plays did not exist there: the
first theatre—called, appropriately enough, The Theatre—
opened its doors in 1576. Plays had been acted for centuries,
however, before the advent of playhouses. During the Middle
Ages the cathedral towns—York, Chester, Coventry—had
spawned their vast cycles of religious plays, mounted as a
matter of religious faith and local pride by the various craft
guilds. Having been sustained by the Old Faith, they gradually petered out because of their formidable cost and, after
Reformation, the hostile official climate of the new dispensation. But at Coventry, only eighteen miles distant from
Stratford, the cycle depicting Biblical events ranging from
Lucifer's fall and Adam's to the Assumption of the Virgin and
finally to Doomsday was still being performed. Shakespeare,
as a boy of fifteen, may have seen them acted, for verbal
echoes from the Mysteries find their way into the secular
plays he later wrote for the London companies.

Pageantry, associated with dramatic or quasi-dramatic en-
tertainments, accompanied the Queen in progress time.
"When it pleaseth her in the summer season to recreate
herself abroad," a contemporary observed, "and view the
estate of the country, every nobleman's house is her palace."
Come July, she would lock the gates of her London palaces
and, with her gorgeously bedecked retinue, journey into the
countryside, there to view her subjects and be viewed by
them. Thus did she combine holiday and public relations.
Hygiene and economy too. Having fouled its own nest, the
Court moved on at regular intervals to more wholesome
abodes. Elaborate preparations, costing thousands of pounds,
preceded the Queen's arrival. Workmen pitched tents, dug
pits, and excavated lakes. Costumes, musicians, and fireworks
were laid on; lavish gifts were bestowed. Elizabeth went
often to Nonsuch, the pleasure palace her father had built
with the spoil of monasteries. Her favorite, the Earl of
Arundel, Steward of the Queen's household, was (by royal
grant) the master of Nonsuch. Tongues wagged that the
Queen would marry him, but he had to vie with other
favorites, among them Robert Dudley, the Earl of Leicester. At
Kenilworth Castle, situated "as it were in the navel of
England" a dozen miles from Stratford, Leicester entertained
his monarch magnificently for nineteen days in the summer
of 1575. He was, after all, her favorite favorite.

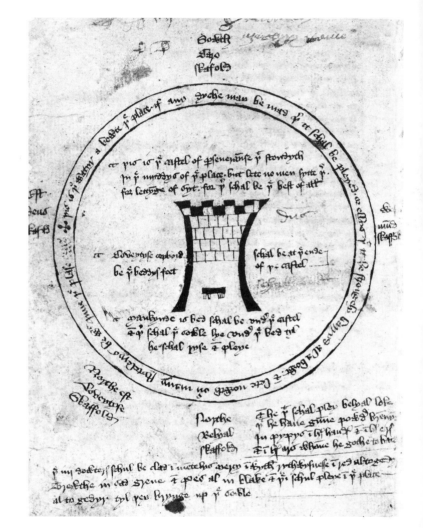

Left: *Title page and detail from George Turberville's BOOKE OF FAULCONRIE OR HAUKING (London, 1575).*
Right: *According to the elaborate ritual of the royal hunt, Queen Elizabeth is presented with a knife to make the first cut into a slain deer. A woodcut in George Turberville's NOBLE ARTE OF VENERIE OR HUNTING (London, 1575).*

An eyewitness account of the princely pleasures of Kenilworth describes a water pageant in the spacious lake on the castle grounds. Arion appeared on the back of a dolphin transported by a boat with oars simulating fins. Also in the waters swam a mermaid, eighteen feet long, with Triton alongside. To the music of instrumentalists inside the dolphin's belly, Arion sang (so a gentleman usher present enthused) "a delectable ditty of a song well apted to a melodious noise." During these festivities, as the local populace pressed in to catch glimpses of the Queen and the fireworks, the floating island and the pageants, were Alderman Shakespeare and his eleven-year-old son among them? A beguiling fancy made the more beguiling by a strangely fanciful passage in *A Midsummer Night's Dream.* "Thou rememb'rest," Oberon puts Puck in mind,

> Since once I sat upon a promontory,
> And heard a mermaid on a dolphin's back
> Uttering such dulcet and harmonious breath
> That the rude sea grew civil at her song,
> And certain stars shot madly from their spheres
> To hear the sea-maid's music.

Just possibly—and one should claim no more than possibility—Oberon's creator himself, as an awe-struck boy, heard the song sung from a dolphin's back one midsummer night in his own Warwickshire.

Around the same time that the aristocracy was disporting itself with princely pleasures at Kenilworth, John Shakespeare set in motion, with the College of Arms, the machinery for procuring armorial bearings. A coat of arms would demonstrate, more forcibly than wealth, the social status achieved by a humble tenant farmer's son. But John never followed through with his application. He had other things on his mind. Inexorably his fortunes declined: he borrowed money, parted with lands out of necessity, kept from church "for fear of process for debt." Eventually his corporation brethren chose another alderman to replace him, for he had long since ceased attending council meetings. What lay behind John Shakespeare's reversals the historical records fail to disclose, but an economic recession gripped the Midlands in those years. Others suffered more grievously. The poor naked wretches whose lot Shakespeare so compassionately evokes in *King Lear* represent the darker side of the Warwickshire world in which he grew up.

William's schooldays ended. According to the report of an early biographer, "the narrowness of his circumstances, and the want of his assistance at home, forced his father to withdraw him" from the Stratford grammar school. Presumably, then, he helped his father in his glove business for a time. He also married. At eighteen Shakespeare took as his bride the daughter of a yeoman of Shottery, only a mile from Stratford; Anne Hathaway's Cottage, picturesquely thatched, still stands. She was eight years older than the youthful groom, and pregnant. Her condition rendered delay awkward, so the ecclesiastical authorities at nearby Worcester granted the couple permission to solemnize matrimony with only one asking of the banns—rather than the customary three. Biographers have sniffed the aroma of gunshot, but William, as a minor, could not have wed without parental approval. On May 26, 1583, a daughter, Susanna, was baptized in Holy Trinity, followed, less than two years later, on February 2, 1585, by the christening of twins, Hamnet and Judith. William Shakespeare's family was complete.

All he required now was a career. We do not hear of Shakespeare in London until seven years later. Just when, and under what circumstances, he joined the stage, history has not revealed. This is the phase of his life we call the Lost Years. A venerable legend holds that the master of Charlecote apprehended Shakespeare poaching, and used him so badly that the malefactor penned a bitter ballad; whereupon Sir Thomas redoubled his prosecution, until at length William left his family and business in Stratford to find shelter in the capital. A more likely, and only slightly less romantic, possibility is that Shakespeare joined a troupe of actors passing through Warwickshire. When the Queen's Men stopped in Stratford in 1587, they were short a man, William Knell having been lately killed in a brawl with a fellow actor. Maybe Shakespeare took Knell's place and thus found his way to London and stage-land.

For find his way he did; the years of triumph comprise another chapter in his career to which we shall shortly turn. Suffice it here to note that, unlike many artists in all ages, Shakespeare did not turn his back on his provincial roots. In Stratford his family remained. His children married in Stratford church, and his grandchildren were christened there. In time he and his wife would lie buried in the chancel. Before then he had demonstrated to his fellow townsmen that he was a man of substance and position, for the sublime poet did not disdain such mundane rewards.

On the threshold of his most astonishing creative success, Shakespeare renewed his father's application for a grant of arms. This the College of Heralds awarded in 1596. In this way Shakespeare obtained the familiar shield displaying a spear, with a falcon for a crest. Three years later another grant authorized the Shakespeares to combine their arms with those of the Ardens, but in the end they decided against the impaling. In a curious episode in 1602 the Shakespeare grants stirred up a tempest of teapot proportions at the College. The York Herald, Ralph Brooke, who was quarreling with other

Below: *The highly decorated facade of Nonsuch Palace, a vignette from the map of Surrey in John Speed's atlas, THEATRUM IMPERII MAGNAE BRITANNIAE (London, 1616).*

Right: *Queen Elizabeth, here shown (above) in an open coach as she proceeds in state to Nonsuch Palace in Surrey, one of her favorite country residences. Architecturally one of the most elaborate of royal palaces, Nonsuch (middle) was famous for its brightly painted and gilded facade. The women (below) typify aristocratic dress of the period. All three illustrations derive from an engraving by the Flemish artist Georg Hoefnagel around 1582.*

Bottom: *Windsor Castle from the north, as it appeared about 1579, in a view by Georg Hoefnagel. Windsor was then a country castle with nearby woodlands where Queen Elizabeth could hunt. The village of Windsor, where Shakespeare set his MERRY WIVES OF WINDSOR, nestles under the castle to the right.*

officials there, drew up a list of twenty-three instances in which, he felt, they had abused their prerogatives. "Shakespeare the Player" appears fourth, below a rough sketch of his arms. No doubt the term *player* has a derisive application. Players did not then rate with the best people.

Let that pass. Nothing came of the complaint, and meanwhile Shakespeare had acquired the second biggest house in Stratford. The biggest house was not then up for sale. That was in 1597. Two months after the transaction, the vendor, William Underhill, met with an unfortunate accident: his first-born son, Fulke, poisoned him. Fulke paid for his crime by being hanged at Warwick in 1599. When his younger brother Hercules reached his majority in 1602, Shakespeare protected his title to New Place by having him reconfirm the transfer. The document now in the Folger Library is one of two there which we may with some confidence assume were once in Shakespeare's own keeping.

The legal Latin of the Underhill reconfirmation describes Shakespeare's property as having "duobus horreis duobus gardinis et duobus pomariis cum pertinenciis"—two barns, two gardens, and two orchards, with appurtenances. A plausible tradition holds that, after retiring from the stage, Shakespeare passed the twilight of his days cultivating his garden. The art of gardening was, in his times, highly developed, as treatises such as Thomas Hill's *Gardener's Labyrinth* and William Lawson's *New Orchard and Garden* testify. These manuals advise on "the choice of seeds, apt times for sowing, setting, planting, and watering, and the vessels and instruments serving to that use and purpose." They illustrate the worthy ordering of "dainty herbs, delectable flowers, pleasant fruits, and fine roots." They show how to beautify gardens with knots and mazes, and describe grafting, bee husbandry, and other associated skills. The author of *The Winter's Tale* knew something of the art which the gardener, like the poet, must share with great creating nature. "You see, sweet maid," the disguised Polixenes lectures Perdita, decked like Flora herself in flowers of the season,

> we marry
> A gentler scion to the wildest stock,
> And make conceive a bark of baser kind
> By bud of nobler race. This is an art
> Which does mend nature—change it rather; but
> The art itself is nature.

Above: *A PERSPECTIVE VIEW OF THE NEW PLACE*, drawing by John Jordan, a local, self-educated Shakespeare enthusiast. Dated 1793, years after the second largest house in Stratford was demolished, Jordan's sketch shows New Place on the left, the Guild Hall and Grammar School in the center, and a portion of the Falcon Inn on the right. Below: *FINAL CONCORD (1602). A* legal document actually once in Shakespeare's hands, this indenture confirmed that Hercules Underhill had deeded his Stratford house, New Place, to William Shakespeare.

Below: *THE GARDENERS LABYRINTH (London, 1586), an early gardening manual by Thomas Hill, shows a walled garden with a pleasant leafy arbor, plots for flowers, and gardeners at work pruning and trimming.*
Opposite page: *A mulberry tree in the herbal DE STIRPIUM (Strassburg, 1552) by Hieronymus Bock. The woodcut by the German artist David Kandel shows the role of the mulberry tree in the Pyramus and Thisbe legend, which figures in A MIDSUMMER NIGHT'S DREAM. The mulberry tree is also associated with Shakespeare, who is said to have had a mulberry tree in his garden at New Place in Stratford. The number of Shakespearean relics that have been carved from the reputed wood of this mulberry tree, which was cut down in 1758, is little short of miraculous.*

The Shakespeare gardens our horticulturists create today derive from the flowers and herbs mentioned in his works rather than from any sketches or descriptions of the grounds of New Place. But Shakespeare's actual garden achieved some local renown, it seems: fifteen years after the dramatist's death, a baronet living in Buckinghamshire instructed one of his men to gather for him some of the fairest buds on the shoots of the last year's vines at New Place. Shakespeare is said to have planted a mulberry there himself. When it was cut down in the eighteenth century, the tree yielded innumerable souvenirs for pilgrims desirous of such secular relics. Thus Shakespeare lives on in carved wood as well as in the pages of his book.

Shakespeare's acquisition of New Place, as well as of his other lands and houses, was made possible by his successful endeavors of art. These he necessarily pursued not in Stratford but in the teeming, thriving metropolis. It is appropriate, therefore, that we now follow the young father of three as, with consequences he could scarcely have foretold, he first took the road from his Warwickshire birthplace to the great capital city.

Pages from A NEW ORCHARD AND GARDEN (London, 1618) by William Lawson. Pictured here (and enlarged on opposite page) is the plan of a small estate such as New Place. The second part of Lawson's book, THE COUNTRY HOUSEWIFES GARDEN, contains information on herbs and plans for intricately planted knot gardens and mazes.

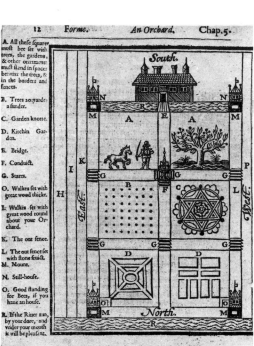

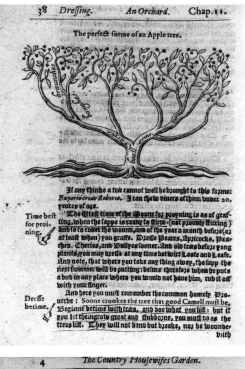

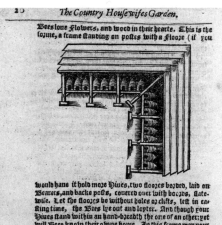

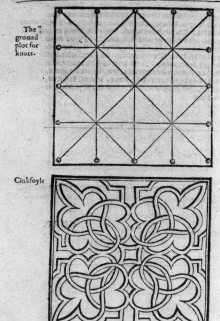

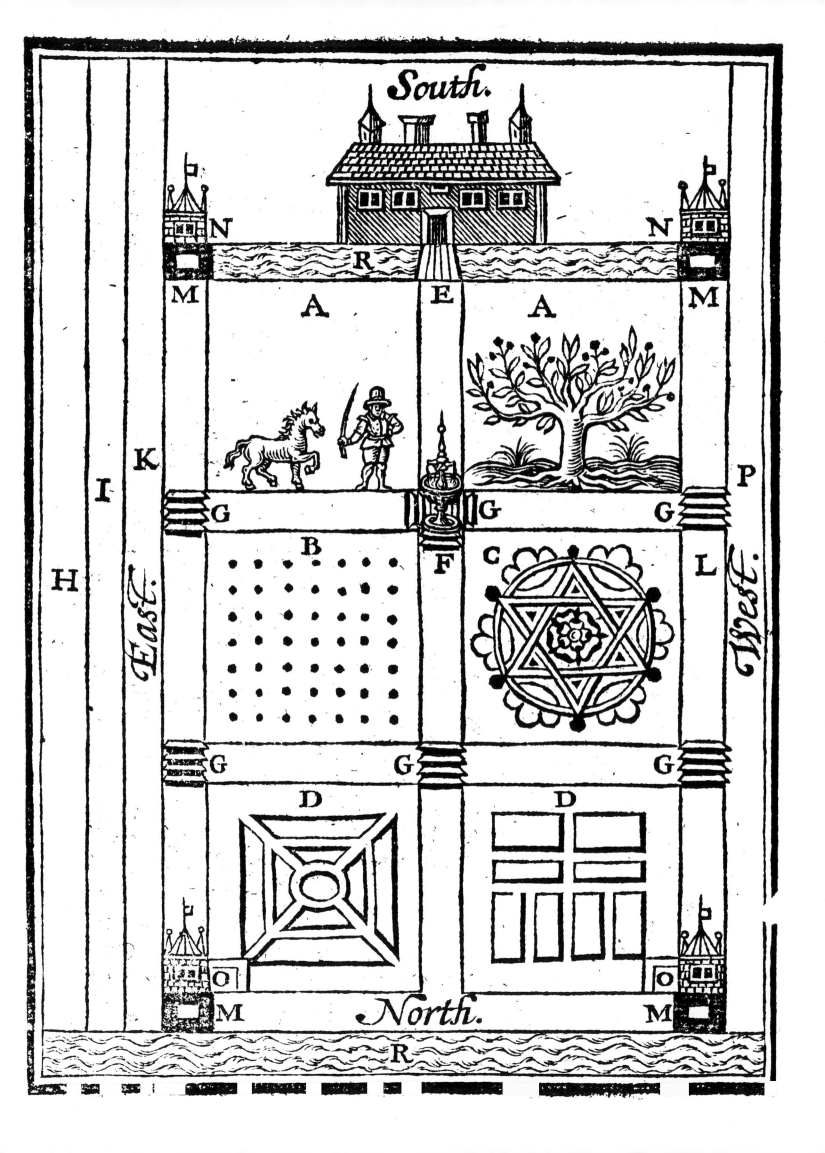

2

The London Years

HORTENSIO....
And tell me now, sweet friend, what happy gale
Blows you to Padua here from old Verona?
PETRUCHIO. Such wind as scatters young men through the
   world
To seek their fortunes farther than at home,
Where small experience grows.

*Queen Elizabeth before Parliament. A
hand-colored engraving in NOBILITAS
POLITICA VEL CIVILIS (London, 1608),
a book on the major dignitaries and
nobles of England by Robert Glover,
Somerset Herald.*

London lay a hundred miles off. Shakespeare may well have traveled on foot—normally a four days' journey—before he had made his name and fortune. He would first cross the stone bridge that a great benefactor of Stratford, Sir Hugh Clopton, built in the fifteenth century, a bridge which stands yet. Then there were two routes to follow. The shorter would take Shakespeare over rolling hills, across treeless downs, and past the royal park, thick with oaks and beeches, of Woodstock. Eventually, along this route, he would see before him the spires of Oxford.

Those who traced the University back to Brute the Trojan, or to the Druids, perhaps somewhat exaggerated its antiquity. But Oxford was, with Cambridge, a venerable seat of learning, respected throughout Europe. Erasmus had lectured there. In Shakespeare's day New College was already old. St. John's College, added in 1555, was a brash newcomer; not until 1571 did the Queen grant a charter for the founding of Jesus College. And it was thirty more years before Sir Thomas Bodley opened with 2,000 volumes the library that would become famous in association with his name. Early in Elizabeth's reign the two universities, which had suffered during the Reformation, were incorporated and reorganized. Statutes (in this period statutes governed almost everything) set forth the duties of the dons, who lectured on theology, civil and ecclesiastical law, medicine, philosophy and dialectic, mathematics, Greek, and Hebrew. The curriculum remained, for the most part, medieval. Had Shakespeare been privileged to attend, he might have improved his Greek, and perhaps added Homer and Euripides, in the original, to the classical vein he would afterward mine. Other dramatists of Shakespeare's generation—Marlowe, Greene, Peele—prided themselves on their academic credentials. Shakespeare would perforce find his way without the distinction of being a University Wit. He missed out, too, on the amateur theatricals that enlivened the Christmas holidays and other special occasions in the college halls. The plays produced, some of which survive, had an academic cast—in both senses of that word. They *were* amateur, whereas Shakespeare would be the most thoroughgoing of professionals.

His company would play often in Oxford when on their provincial circuit. Shakespeare no doubt accompanied them at least some of the time. And, although the records do not disclose which plays were performed, these must have included some titles by the troupe's foremost dramatist. When academic recognition—of a sort—first came to Shakespeare, that happened not at Oxford but at Cambridge. There, in St. John's College, the students acted a dramatic trilogy, the *Parnassus* plays, around the turn of the seventeenth century. In *The Return from Parnassus* Gullio presents himself as an admirer of "sweet Master Shakespeare," whose picture he will have in his study at court and whose *Venus and Adonis* he will keep under his pillow. Since Gullio is (as his name suggests) a fool in a satirical play, the praise is at best equivocal. No matter. It shows that, sometime between 1598 and 1601, Shakespeare's reputation had penetrated the academy's ivy-covered walls.

That was to come: Shakespeare had first to establish himself. The university spires were merely a point of interest along the way of his first journey. High Wycombe and Beaconsfield followed; Uxbridge and Brentford after that. Then, having turned south by St. Giles in the Fields, a rural village, and proceeded into Holborn, he would finally pass through Newgate, and find himself in his city for conquest.

Left: *PROGRESS TO PARNASSUS (ca. 1603),* manuscript copy of a student play acted at St. John's College, Cambridge, in 1603, probably as a part of the Christmas revels. The play shows the students' familiarity with Shakespeare as a playwright. In Act IV, scene iii there is a dialogue between Richard Burbage and Will Kempe, two London actors who appear as characters in the play. Kempe alludes to Shakespeare: "Few of the university men pen plays well; they smell too much of the writer Ovid, and that writer Metamorphoses, and talk too much of Proserpina and Jupiter. Why, here's our fellow Shakespeare puts them all down, ay, and Ben Jonson too. O that Ben Jonson is a pestilent fellow. He brought up Horace giving the poets a pill, but our fellow Shakespeare hath given him a purge that made him bewray his credit." A printed version of the play, entitled *THE RETURNE FROM PARNASSUS,* appeared in 1606.

Right: *Example of a chained binding: a blind-stamped contemporary pigskin cover with brass corners, clasps, and bosses, and a horn-covered inset giving the title of the book. When the art of printing was relatively new and books were very costly, chains were used to attach volumes to shelves. Inside the binding one finds the OPERA ("Works") of Thomas à Kempis, published in Nuremberg in 1494.*

This page: *London Bridge with its many shops and houses, as depicted by John Norden in 1597 in THE VIEW OF LONDON BRIDGE FROM EAST TO WESTE. Decapitated heads are displayed on pikes from the top of the building to the left, while watermen in their boats shoot through the swift waters of the bridge's arches. Only two copies of this 1597 engraving are known, both of them in the Folger collection.*

Opposite page: *Bird's-eye view of London, LONDINUM FERACISSIMI ANG-LIAE REGNI METROPOLIS, from the atlas CIVITATIS ORBIS TERRARUM by Georg Braun (ca. 1574). In Braun's view one can see both banks of the river, as well as the court buildings at Westminster around the curve of the river to the left. The artist seems to have had an eye for taverns, two of which can be seen on either bank of the river at the extreme right.*

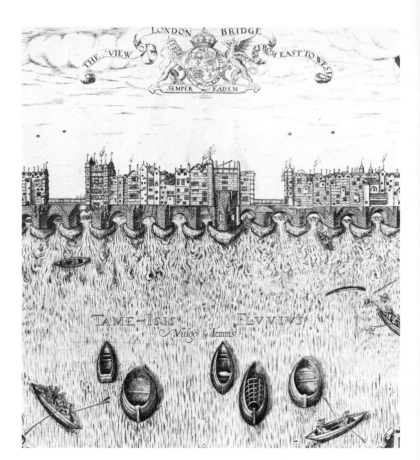

Most of the London that Shakespeare knew would go up in flames in the Great Fire of 1666. Yet his city is familiar enough to the modern armchair traveler. The principal landmarks—the Tower, St. Paul's Cathedral, London Bridge, and the rest—live in Shakespeare's English history plays as backdrops or points of reference. The Eastcheap tavern where Falstaff and Prince Hal and their cronies cavorted becomes, when the houselights dim, our neighborhood pub. Shakespeare's London lives too in the splendid sweep of the panoramas engraved by Claes Jan Visscher and Wenceslaus Hollar. These depict, in lovingly elaborate detail, the metropolis as viewed from Bankside—in the foreground, to the west, the playhouses; a single bridge cluttered with buildings (the Elizabethan equivalent of a shopping plaza) spanning the great tidal river; on the opposite bank the Tower, St. Paul's shorn of its wooden spire (a casualty of lightning), the Blackfriars, the Royal Exchange, innumerable church steeples, huddled tenements, an abundance of trees, and here and there a windmill. On the water, wherries and eel boats hobnob with tall two- and three-masted merchant ships, while the quays and wharves await the discharge of passengers and cargo.

"A man would say that seeth the shipping there," marveled the great Elizabethan antiquary Camden, "that it is, as it were, a very wood of trees disbranched to make glades and let in light: so shaded it is with masts and sails." Thus shaded, the Thames made London the vital center of the realm for trade and commerce.

London was also the center for the book trade. A little way up river, and not then technically part of the metropolis, lay Westminster. Here the courts held their sessions and the legal profession found its nexus. The Inns of Court, where resident students read for the bar, comprised a third university. At Westminster Palace, which (it was said) Edward the Confessor had founded, Parliament met when, as was infrequently the case, Elizabeth summoned it. In Westminster too the Queen kept her court at Whitehall Palace, except when it pleased her to remove to one of her other nearby seats—Richmond or Greenwich or Hampton Court—or ride forth on progress. Sometimes the players, suitably rewarded, acted before her. Elizabeth herself never visited a public theatre, but many thousands paid their pennies to see the leading metropolitan companies perform at the Theatre or the Swan or the Globe. With these attractions and others, London was—then as now—a mecca for foreign visitors.

Yet, by modern standards, the capital of the English Renaissance was hardly more than a modest-sized city. An informed guess would put the population at around 160,000. But of course statistics are relative: no other city of the realm approached London in scale. Statistics may mislead too.

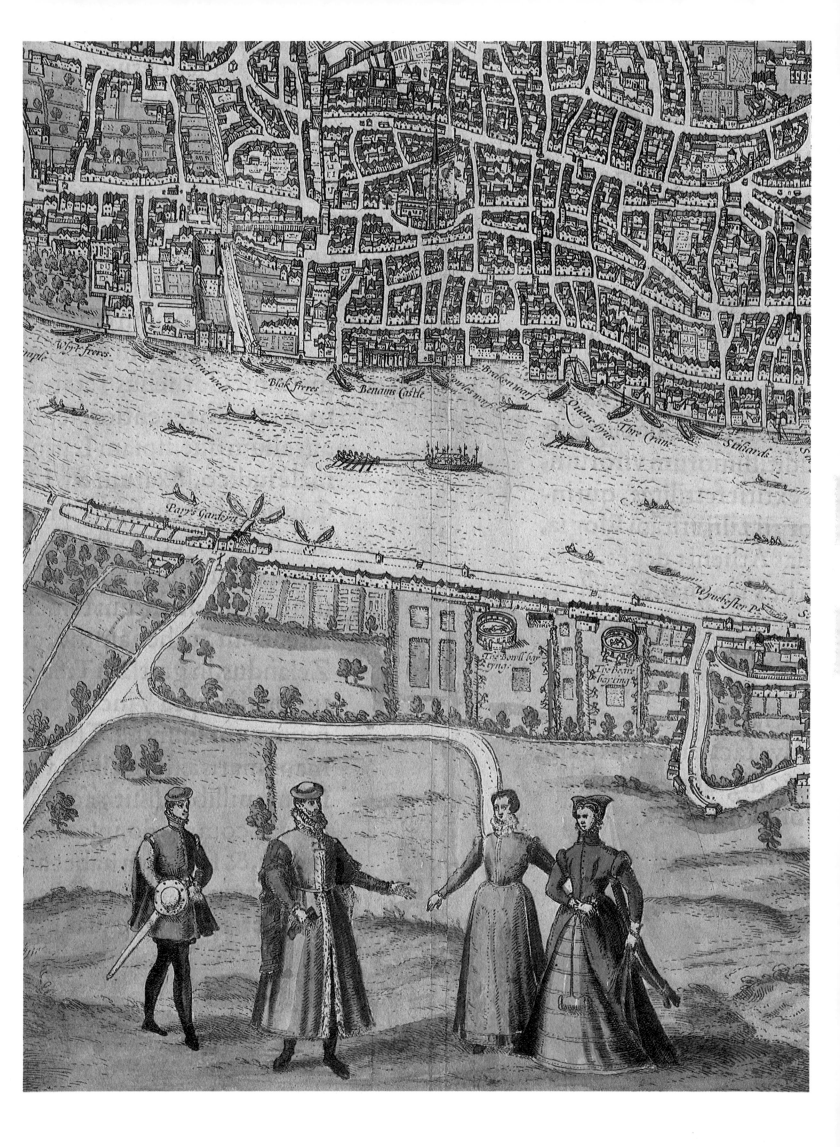

Whyt freres.   Bridwell   Blak freres   Benams Castle   Poules wharf   Brokenwarf   Queen hiue   The Cran   Stiliards

Parys Garden

Wynchester ps.

The Bowll bar Etyng.   The Bear bayting

*LONDINUM FLORENTISSIMA BRITAN-
NIAE URBS, a panoramic view of London from the south, by the Amsterdam
engraver Claes Jansz Visscher.
Visscher's view (here represented in a
variant, ca. 1625, of the original view
of 1616) shows the theatres, St. Paul's
Cathedral, London Bridge, the Tower,
and other major buildings.*

S.Laurens Poultney

DON

The Exchange

The Dutch Churche

S. Michaelis

S. Peter

Leadne Hall

S. Steuen

S. Andrew

S.Dunston

Olde Swan

Stilliaggers hall

The Bridge

F L V I V S.

Winchester howse

S. Mary Oueris

South   Warke.

Urban development sprawled over the ancient city walls in untidy suburbs. Responding to craft-guild pressures and the ever-present threat of plague, the authorities endeavored to contain growth. A proclamation of 1580 declares that the Queen, acting with the "good and deliberate advice of her Council, and being also thereto moved by the considerable opinions of the Lord Mayor, Aldermen, and other grave wise men in and about the city, doth charge and straightly command all manner of persons...to desist and forbear from any new building of any house or tenement within three miles from any of the gates of the said city of London." Such efforts naturally failed, and in due course the suburbs would become part of Greater London. Meanwhile, despite metropolitan expansion, in Shakespeare's day the open country still nestled close in. A short walk along Holborn, past St. Giles's Church, would bring the stroller to open fields; rising country and farmsteads lay beyond the metropolis.

This was the city in which Shakespeare first attracted notice in 1592. The earliest report, unlike all others, is hostile. As he lay dying in pitiful squalor, Robert Greene—poet, rakehell, and Cambridge M.A.—penned his swansong, *Greene's Groatsworth of Wit, Bought with a Million of Repentance*. In better days he had graced the bookstalls with romances—*Pandosto, Menaphon, Tully's Love,* and others— and the theatres with plays, of which one, *Friar Bacon and Friar Bungay,* may be reckoned a minor masterpiece.

Never Too Late is the title of one of Greene's efforts; but for him it *was* too late. On his deathbed, all his possessions pawned, reduced to begging for his pot of malmsey, he could feel only bitter envy for the young Warwickshireman who, without benefit of a university degree, had set up rival shop as a playwright.

A successful playwright. In the *Groatsworth* Greene warns some of his "fellow scholars about this city" of "an upstart crow, beautified with our feathers, that with his *tiger's heart wrapped in a player's hide* supposes he is as well able to bombast out a blank verse as the best of you; and, being an absolute *Johannes Factotum* [i.e. Jack-of-all-trades], is in his own conceit the only Shake-scene in a country." The "tiger's heart" alludes sneeringly to a line in Shakespeare's *3 Henry VI:* "O tiger's heart wrapp'd in a woman's hide!" About the object of Greene's venom there can be no doubt.

Nor can there be any question about the intemperateness of the attack. This was recognized at the time. Shakespeare found a perhaps unexpected champion in Henry Chettle, by trade a printer and by inclination a hack *littérateur* who turned out catchpenny pamphlets and perishable plays. To

Chettle fell the unedifying task of preparing Greene's disordered and almost illegible papers for the press. For better or worse—mainly worse—he bore some responsibility for the finished product. And no sooner had the *Groatsworth of Wit* appeared than he made amends with the handsome apologia prefacing his own *Kind-Heart's Dream.* "I am as sorry," Chettle writes in his preface, "as if the original fault had been my fault, because myself have seen his demeanor no less civil than he excellent in the quality he professes: besides, divers of worship have reported his uprightness of dealing, which argues his honesty, and his facetious grace in writing, that approves his art." The reference to the "quality he professes" is an acknowledgment that Shakespeare served his company not only as a dramatist but also as an actor. This helps account for Greene's sneer at a mere player who dared, like the crow, to imitate his betters. Notwithstanding such audacity, Shakespeare had made friends in high places: the "divers of worship" to whom Chettle alludes. Who were they? Had Shakespeare, as some biographers infer, already found a noble patron? Probably not. Elizabethans made careful distinctions in their forms of address. *Worship* applied to gentlemen; aristocrats Chettle would have described as "divers of honor."

Whoever these supporters were, they remain as anonymous as the multitudes who applauded Shakespeare's plays in Shoreditch, the northern suburb beyond Finsbury fields where the first theatres were built, comfortably outside the purview of the municipal authorities who looked with puritanical disdain on such idle pastimes. Eventually (as we shall see) Shakespeare's company would move across the Thames to the pleasure resorts of Bankside; but in these years Burbage's Theatre was its showcase. Meanwhile, by the early nineties, Shakespeare had established himself as a potent force in a burgeoning new industry, having already demonstrated his youthful mastery of the several genres: history with the *Henry VI* plays, tragedy with *Titus Andronicus,* and comedy with *The Taming of the Shrew* and *The Comedy of Errors.*

The distinctive power of *1 Henry VI* is evoked by a contemporary, Thomas Nashe. He describes the effect on audiences of the death of Talbot, left by rivalrous peers to die valiantly on a forsaken field in France:

> How would it have joyed brave Talbot (the terror of the French) to think that after he had lain two hundred years in his tomb, he should triumph again on the stage, and have his bones new embalmed with the tears of ten thousand spectators at least (at several times), who, in the tragedian that represents his person, imagine they behold him fresh bleeding.

A famous early reference to Shake-speare as an upstart crow in GREENES GROATS-WORTH OF WITTE (London, 1592). The author, Robert Greene, was a prolific profligate, original editions of whose works are now very scarce.

pendeſt on ſo meane a ſtay. Baſe minded men all three of you, if by my miſerie you be not warnd: for vnto none of you (like mee) ſought thoſe burres to cleaue : thoſe Puppets (I meane) that ſpake from our mouths, thoſe Anticks garniſht in our colours. Is it not ſtrange, that I, to whom they all haue beene beholding: is it not like that you, to whome they all haue beene beholding, ſhall (were yee in that caſe as I am now) bee both at once of them forſaken? Yes truſt them not : for there is an vp-ſtart Crow, beautified with our feathers, that with his *Tygers hart wrapt in a Players hyde*, ſuppoſes he is as well able to bombaſt out a blanke verſe as the beſt of you : and beeing an abſolute *Iohannes fac totum*, is in his owne conceit the onely Shake-ſcene in a countrey. O that I might intreat your rare wits to be imploied in more profitable courſes : & let thoſe Apes imitate your paſt excellence, and neuer more acquaint them with your admired inuentions. I knowe the beſt huſband of

These tears were all shed in the playhouse, not the study; for none of Shakespeare's plays had yet seen print. That would shortly come, without his consent or approval. As for now, his days were spent in the service of his troupe, whichever that was: Strange's Men, perhaps, or the Queen's. He found his creative fulfillment in performance rather than in publication.

During his idle hours he could plunge into the life of the town. London, which conferred no degrees, became his university, providing the non-academic context for that knowledge of the human heart, unrivaled in range and depth, which for many remains the most astonishing aspect of the Shakespearean achievement. Around him he could see a fair city full of folk, and observe the inexhaustible pageant of everyday life.

There is a scene in *1 Henry VI* in which Joan La Pucelle (whom we better remember as Joan of Arc) gains entrance into Rouen for her soldiers by having them dress like countrymen, with sacks upon their backs. When the watch asks who goes, she answers for her men, "poor market-folks that come to sell their corn." Taken in, he opens the gates. "Enter, go in; the market-bell is rung." Shakespeare had seen the country folk with their wares, on foot or in their carts, and he had heard the market bell ring. To Grace Church Street (so named from "the parish church of St. Benet, called Grass Church, of the herb-market there kept") husbandmen brought corn and malt to sell at their standings in the great corn market which, from the Middle Ages, had gone on there. Blacksmiths, too, openly hawked their wares on the pavement of Grace Church market. At the Market hill (near Pepper Alley in Long Southwark) leather changed hands. The Stocks, in Cornhill Ward, were a market place for flesh and fish. Billingsgate, one of the main city wharves, also offered freshly caught fish, but not until much later—in 1696—did Parliament allow daily market there. In Shakespeare's time it was still "an open place for the landing and bringing in of any fish, corn, salt stores, victuals, and fruit (grocery wares excepted)." A small portion of Smithfield was reserved, as in times past, for marketing horses and cattle. Bakewell Hall, in the little ward of Bassings Hall, was immemorially "employed as a weekly market place for all sorts of woollen clothes broad and narrow, brought from all parts of this realm, there to be sold." Farmers fetched their poultry to Leaden Hall market, where other commerce went on as well. Simon Eyre, the draper celebrated by Thomas Dekker in *The Shoemakers' Holiday,* had in 1445 built a granary at his own expense in Leaden Hall, and the market was also used for canvas and woolens. John Stow, who knew and loved every corner of Elizabethan London, remembered the Leaden Hall of his youth. The

description in his *Survey of London* gives us some sense of the organization of an Elizabethan market:

> In a part of the north quadrant on the east side of the north gate, was the common beams for weighing of wool and other wares, as had been accustomed. On the west side of the gate was the scales to weigh meal. The other three sides were reserved for the most part to the making and resting of the pageants showed at Midsummer in the watch. The remnants of the sides and quadrants were employed for the stowage of wool sacks, but not closed up. The lofts above were partly used by the painters in working for the decking of pageants and other devices, for beautifying of the watch and watchmen; the residue of the lofts were letten out to merchants, the wool-winders and packers therein to wind and pack their wools.

These, among others, were the London markets. But tradesmen and sellers of wares kept shops everywhere: mercers and haberdashers on London Bridge, goldsmiths in Cheapside, pepperers and grocers in Bucklersbury, drapers in Candlewick Street, skinners in Bridge Row, stockfish-mongers, cooks, and ironmongers in Thames Street, poulterers in Grace Street—while "the brewers for the most part remained near to the friendly waters of the Thames." Shops sprouted even in the ancient city wall, the curriers having their premises in the wall near Moorgate. In the old days the bakers of London were enjoined to sell no bread in shops or houses: only in the market in Bread Street. Such centralization had long since vanished in the wake of urban growth, but in a regulated economy nothing is more stringently controlled than the price and quality of our daily bread. Stow records how, in the reign of Edward IV, a baker named John of Stratford (that is, Stratford-le-Bow) "for making bread lesser than the assize, was with a fool's hood on his head, and loaves of bread about his neck, drawn on a hurdle through the streets of this city." Elizabeth's Privy Council still enforced the "statutes and ancient customs for making and retailing of all lawful sorts of bread."

In Elizabethan England the Crown sought, also, to curb excess in apparel. Not very successfully; fashion too enjoyed a renaissance, reveling in luxurious materials (silks and velvets from Italy and France) ornamented with precious jewels among the fashionable. The shapes of garments became fantasticated. Invented by a Spanish princess, the farthingale—a hooped petticoat covered with taffeta and worn under skirts—was introduced at the French court, as the *verdugale,* in the sixteenth century. Transplanted into England, it had grown, as the sixteenth century waned, into the huge cartwheel farthingale, as wide at hem as at hip. The ruff too had commenced modestly as a simple frill encircling the neck when Catherine de Medici wore it in 1533 for her

Crumenarius. Der Seckler.

Imperiosa iugo quemcunq, pecunia subdit,
Et custos auri vis bonus esse tui.
Huc properes, gressuq, pet.as fora nostra citato,
Hic oculos etiam quod tibi pascat, erit.

Ecce tibi varia loculos è pelle ferarum,
Distinctos habitu multicolore damus,
Millibus è multis nunc emptor amice crumenis,
Elige marsupium quod tibi cunq, placet.
Mille quod impletum fuluis tamen opto monetis
Splendeat; & fidus sit comes vsq tibi.

K 2   Ligula-

Opposite page: *A glover and purse-maker's shop as depicted in Hartmann Schopper's* PANOPLIA OMNIUM ILLIBERALIUM MECHANICARUM AUT SEDENTARIUM ARTIUM GENERA CONTINENS *(Frankfurt-am-Main, 1568), a woodcut book treating the various arts and crafts of the sixteenth century. Since his father was a glover, Shakespeare would have been well acquainted with this trade.*

Below: *THE ASSISE OF BREAD (London, 1600). This utilitarian listing represents an early form of consumer protection, setting the price of bread according to the market price of wheat as given in the tables.*

{ God blesseth true labour With plentie and fauour. } { Be still quicke and kinde Reward thou shalt finde. } { Pricke out at thy plesure But in tru honest mesure } { Be watchfull and wise In goodnes to rise. }

The weight of the peny white Lofe according to the corse Cocket. An.51.H.3.	The weight of the halfe peny wheaton Lofe drawne frō the corse coket. A.51.H.3	The weight of the peny wheaton Lofe drawne frō the corse Cocket An.51.H.3.	The weight of the peny houshold Lofe drawne frō the corse Cocket. An.51.H.3.
viij ℥ q.	vj.℥.iij.ꝺ.	xij.℥.q.i.ꝺ.	xvj.℥.ꝺi.
viij.℥.iij ꝺ.	vj.℥.ij.ꝺ.	xij.℥.iiij.ꝺ.	xvj.℥.q.i.ꝺ.
vij.℥.j ꝺ.	vj.℥.	xij.℥.	xvj.℥.ij.ꝺ.
vij.℥.iij.q.iij.ꝺ.	v.℥.iij.q.iiij.ꝺ.	xi.℥.iij.q.iij.ꝺ.	ꝺv.℥.iij.q.i.ꝺ.
vij.℥ iij.q ij.ꝺ.	v.℥.iij.q.iij.ꝺ.	xj.℥.iij.q.i.ꝺ.	ꝺv.℥.ꝺi.iiij.ꝺ.
vij.℥.iij q.	v.℥.iij.q.j.ꝺ.	xj.℥.ꝺi.ij.ꝺ.	ꝺv.℥.ꝺi.
vij.℥.ꝺi iij.ꝺ.	v.℥.iij.q.	xj.℥.ꝺi.	ꝺv.℥.q.j.ꝺ.
vij ℥.ꝺi.ij.ꝺ.	v.℥.ꝺi.iij.ꝺ.	ꝺj.℥.q.j.ꝺ.	ꝺv.℥.iij.ꝺ.
vij ℥ ꝺi.	v.℥.ꝺi.ij.ꝺ.	ꝺj.℥.iiij.ꝺ.	ꝺv.℥.
vij.℥.q.iij.ꝺ.	v.℥.ꝺi.j.ꝺ.	ꝺj.℥.ij.ꝺ.	xiij.℥.iij.q.j.ꝺ.

Below: *Leaves from a proclamation against "excesses in apparel" forbidding the wearing of excessively long cloaks and great ruffs. It was issued by Queen Elizabeth on February 12, 1580. Opposite page: Courtier and his lady. Anonymous watercolor costume sketch from the time of James I.*

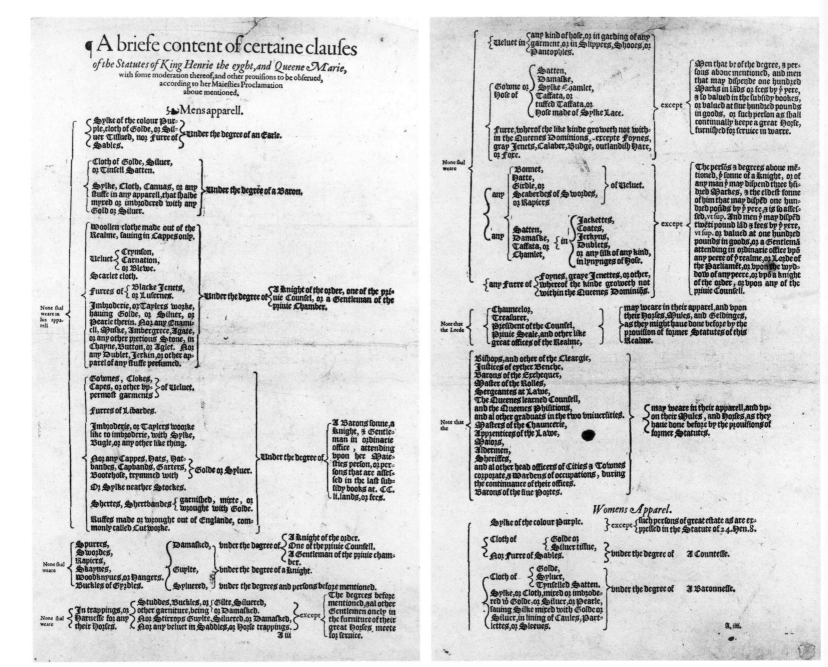

wedding to Henry II of France. In England ruffs quickly became the fashion. Simple linen gave way to cambric or lawn as more amenable to stiffening; Dutch women found themselves in demand to instruct the English in the art of starching. Ruffs grew enormously, the ostentation of size being matched by that of ornamentation: "they are either clogged with gold, silver, or silk lace of stately price, wrought all over with needle work, speckled and sparkled here and there with the sun, the moon, the stars, and many other antiquities strange to behold." So wrote a Puritan moralist in 1583. A generation earlier, in 1562, Elizabeth had issued an edict prohibiting the wearing of great ruffs; in 1597 she tried again, commanding that "no person shall use or wear such great and excessive ruffs, in or about the uppermost parts of their necks." Despite such injunctions, her subjects resisted leaving off "such fond, disguised and monstrous manner of attiring themselves."

If ruffs were in, breasts too were in—or, to be more precise, out—décolletage being fashionable. For the rest, men and women squashed their upper torsos into close-fitting doublets stiffened with wood or metal or whalebone. This gesture in the direction of austerity they mitigated with huge padded and bejeweled leg-of-mutton sleeves. Ladies wore costly embroidered gloves, lined with fur, and carried fans (an Italian innovation) attached to the points of their stomachers—the ornamental covering on the front part of the bodice. Some fans contained small mirrors; others had handles of gold or silver inlaid with precious stones. Ladies favored pointed shoes. On horseback they wore masks. They dyed their hair and painted their faces, despite pulpit denunciations of such depravity. The disapproval, which may strike moderns living in a cosmetic age as odd, was amply justified by the health hazards make-up posed. For the basic white of all sixteenth-century cosmetics derived from lead, and lead poisoning might—and sometimes did—result from the quest for artificial beauty. "I have heard of your paintings too, well enough," Hamlet chastises Ophelia: "God hath given you one face, and you make yourselves another." Ophelia, in turn, sadly notes that Hamlet is so far gone that he walks about with "doublet all unbrac'd" and "No hat upon his head." Hats were meant to be worn, indoors and out; only in

the presence of royalty did etiquette require a man to be unbonneted. "Put your bonnet to his right use," Hamlet reminds Osric, " 'tis for the head." Fine silk or yarn stockings were in fashion by 1580. Cross-gartering—that is, wearing garters both above and below the knee—was an extravagance calculated to raise eyebrows. Malvolio, in *Twelfth Night,* is tricked into making a fool of himself by donning yellow stockings, cross-gartered.

"And now, my honey love," Petruchio promises Kate in *The Taming of the Shrew,*

> Will we return unto thy father's house
> And revel it as bravely as the best,
> With silken coats and caps, and golden rings,
> With ruffs and cuffs and farthingales and things,
> With scarfs and fans and double change of brav'ry,
> With amber bracelets, beads, and all this knav'ry.

With such accoutrements did the upper classes revel it bravely. Sober bourgeois Londoners exercised greater sartorial restraint. A merchant's wife, even if well-to-do, would usually content herself with a fitted bodice and a plain long gown over her bell-shaped farthingale, while her husband, in his small round cloth cap, would favor a calf-length cloak, sashed at the waist and trimmed with fur. "Certes of all estates," Harrison notes with satisfaction, "our merchants do least alter their attire, and therefore are most to be commended; for albeit that which they wear be very fine and costly, yet in form and color it representeth a great piece of the ancient gravity appertaining to citizens and burgesses." All estates, and both sexes, managed without underwear. Come winter and cold weather, the ladies made do with extra petticoats, and the men put on more shirts. That is, those who could afford them. If the upper classes consumed conspicuously, and the mercantile classes with balance-sheet moderation, many in this period lacked any means at all. They wore rags.

High and low, whether in tatters or in finery, thronged to the capital. Refugees found their way from the religious wars on the Continent. Others, country folk, had been uprooted by the agrarian revolution, known as the enclosure movement, which converted the arable strips of tenant farmers into pasturage. Thus (as Sir Thomas More had bitterly remarked) did sheep devour men. Some of the uprooted and disinherited thrived by virtue of their special skills: the engraver who made our only validated likeness of Shakespeare, as well as the tomb-maker who fashioned his monument in Stratford Church, came of Netherlandish stock resettled in London. Other newcomers found employment as laborers or domestic servants.

Countrywoman (this page) *and other costumes* (opposite page) *from the time of James I. Miniature contemporary watercolors.*

Not everybody was so fortunate. There were masterless men unable to work "without extreme pains, by reason their sinews are so benumbed and stiff through idleness, as their limbs being put to any hard labor will grieve them beyond measure: so they will rather hazard their lives than work." So a Somersetshire Justice of the Peace observed in 1596. These unfortunates became rogues or vagabonds. Like the Counterfeit Crank depicted by Thomas Harmon in his *Caveat or Warning for Commen Cursetors,* they applied to the Upright Man—a master rogue—who initiated them into the thieving brotherhood by pouring a "gage of bowse" (a quart pot of drink) over their pates. Swallowed up by the seamy underside of London life, the world of nips and foists, tavern-haunters and brothel-keepers, they cheated and stole. Plunging into the bohemian underworld of the great city, Robert Greene had surfaced to expose its evils in a series of muckraking pamphlets. These show how country innocents, apprentices, and other such dupes (called conies) are preyed upon by confidence men: the setter, who entices the intended victim; the verser, who disarms suspicion; the barnacle, who tempts the cony to try his luck. Not to mention the rest of the thieving fraternity, each with his own specialty: the cross-biter (swindler), the priggar (horse-stealer), the nip (cutpurse), the foist (pickpocket), as well as the warp, the curber, and the marker, who contributed their specialized skills as lookouts, stealers of household stuff (dexterously using hooks to poke from below into windows), and receivers of stolen goods.

"Truly, sir," pleads Pompey the bawd to the magistrate in *Measure for Measure,* "I am a poor fellow that would live." The number of such poor fellows was augmented by demobilized soldiers, some maimed on the field. In *Henry V,* Pistol, exposed and humiliated after Agincourt, makes plans for a new career:

> Old I do wax; and from my weary limbs
> Honour is cudgell'd. Well, bawd I'll turn,
> And something lean to cutpurse of quick hand.
> To England will I steal, and there I'll steal;
> And patches will I get unto these cudgell'd scars,
> And swear I got them in the Gallia wars.

Others made similar resolutions. The "vagrom men," as they are characterized in *Much Ado About Nothing,* risked imprisonment in the stocks or worse: being whipped, then branded with a hot iron "through the gristle of the right ear," or transported to the American colonies (in the event sometimes a blessing in disguise). A worse fate awaited the second offender: as a felon, he risked the hangman's noose.

Left: *A night watchman or bellman making his rounds and calling the hours, as shown on the title page to Thomas Dekker's THE BELMAN OF LONDON (1608). Dekker's book defines various kinds of villains, rogues, and vagabonds and offers a glossary of underworld slang terms.*

Top right: *Robert Greene's NOTABLE DISCOVERY OF COOSENAGE (London, 1592) describes the methods used by the confidence men of London's underworld to beguile their victims, called conies in Elizabethan slang. Since "cony" was another word for rabbit, the rabbit in the title page*

woodcut displays various gambling devices.
Bottom right: *In this woodcut from Thomas Harman's A CAVEAT OR WARENING FOR COMMEN CURSE-TORS (London, 1567), an actual figure of the Elizabethan underworld, Nicolas Blunt (alias Nicolas Gennings), is*

shown as an upright man (a chief among vagabonds) and as a counterfeit crank (a beggar pretending to be afflicted with falling sickness or some other fearsome disease).

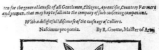

Seventeenth-century miniature water-
colors showing a litter closed (above)
and open (below), a popular mode of
transportation in the time of James I.

The cries of the poor, counterpointed by the clacking of their clap-dishes, filled the streets. But this clamor had to compete with other appeals. Shopkeepers in their entrance-ways called "What do you lack?" Ballad-mongers sang the latest offerings, merry or doleful, or merely informative. That rogue Autolycus, snapper-up of unconsidered trifles in *The Winter's Tale,* boasts an especially engaging item:

> Here's another ballad, of a fish that appeared upon the coast on Wednesday the fourscore of April, forty thousand fathom above water, and sung this ballad against the hard hearts of maids. It was thought she was a woman, and was turn'd into a cold fish for she would not exchange flesh with one that lov'd her. The ballad is very pitiful, and as true.

The samphire collectors, alluded to in *King Lear,* offered their rock samphire (used as a condiment in salads or pickled) dangerously fetched from Dover cliffs. Others hawked hot peas or oatcakes, whiting, or small coals:

> Brooms for old shoes! pouch-rings, boots and buskings!
>   Will ye buy any new brooms?
> New oysters! new oysters! new new cockels!
>   Cockels nigh! fresh herrings! Will ye buy any straw?
>   Ha' ye any kitchen stuff, maids?
>   Pippins fine, cherry ripe, ripe, ripe!
>   Cherry ripe! etc.

Church bells summoned the faithful to prayer. Through the hubbub water-bearers, towels on their shoulders, fetched their tankards. Liveried servants carried their human burdens in sedan chairs. Coaches, introduced to London from Holland around the year of Shakespeare's birth, splashed mud as they hurtled by in the narrow cobbled streets. "The coachman rideth behind the horse tails, lasheth them, and looketh not behind him," Stow protested; "the drayman sitteth and sleepeth on his dray and letteth his horse lead him home." By 1601 gallants had made coaches so popular that the House of Lords saw fit to pass a bill restraining their superfluous use.

Of the magnets drawing the hurrying throngs, one or two are especially conspicuous. Fronting the Cornhill stood the gigantic emporium that Sir Thomas Gresham, a mercer of London, had commissioned Flemish architects to build in imitation of the great Bourse at Antwerp. On January 21, 1571, the Queen herself, attended by her court, had come to the opening and (so Stow writes) "caused the same bourse, by an herald and a trumpet, to be proclaimed the 'Royal Exchange,' and so to be called from thenceforth, and not otherwise." Thus it was. In the cloistered piazza of the Exchange merchants gathered to conduct their affairs while above, in the Pawn, tradesmen—milliners, haberdashers, armorers, apothecaries, glass-sellers, and the rest—carried on

the retail business in shops illuminated by wax-lights. Here one went for a mousetrap, a birdcage, a shoehorn, a lantern, or a Jew's-harp. At the Royal Exchange, Mammon had his London temple.

If one preferred God, St. Paul's beckoned, although Mammon had established a foothold there too. To the Middle Aisle of Paul's, called Duke Humphrey's Walk, repaired the Westminster crowd—courtiers, wits, and gallants about town—to strut in their finery, observe and be observed. Masterless men here set up their bills for service ("I bought him in Paul's," Falstaff says of Bardolph). Lawyers, stationed at their pillars, received clients. Wenches, masks clapped to their faces, arranged assignations. Meanwhile, divine services went on, the choristers keeping a corner of their eyes open for gentry wearing spurs, who would be obliged to pay them spur-money. In previous days Paul's had presented an even more scandalous spectacle: men laden with baskets of bread and vessels of ale had led mules and other beasts through the nave. That went on until 1554, when the Mayor and Common Council levied fines on the use of Paul's for such "unreverent" purposes.

The human scene remained rich enough to engage a playwright's vigilant eye. The churchyard, however, would have held even more beguiling attractions for Shakespeare. There, at the sign of the Greyhound or Holy Ghost or Spread Eagle or whatever, flourished the book trade—a relatively new industry.

In England printing from movable type was less than a century old when Shakespeare was born. In the autumn of 1476, William Caxton, a retired cloth-trader and diplomat, had set up the first English press in the precincts of Westminster Abbey. Then in his middle fifties, Caxton had learned the new craft in Cologne; the craft invented at Strassburg in the late 1430s and perfected by the goldsmith Johann Gutenberg fifteen years later at Mainz. In Bruges, Caxton trained a staff and set up a press from which, in 1474, he issued the first book ever printed in the English language, *The Recuyell of the Histories of Troy.* Back in England, as editor and publisher, Caxton printed for the first time Gower, Chaucer, Lydgate, and Malory, as well as his own prolific writings in prose and verse. But his masterpiece is the edition of *The Canterbury Tales* he brought out in 1478. In the words of George Painter, his biographer, "As a first printing of a national poem in the fifteenth century this is comparable only to the first edition of the *Divina Commedia* (1472) or Villon (1489), and for the monumental magnificence of the type page combined with the ever-new impact and wonder of the text this is perhaps Caxton's finest book."

Once established, printing quickly became a great industry. It was regulated by the Worshipful Company of Stationers on the model of the established craft guilds. Aware of the power of the printed word, the Crown commanded that any book, "of what sort, nature, or in what language soever it be," be licensed in writing before publication. Elizabeth's subjects had no First Amendment rights; in a famous passage of his Sonnets, Shakespeare speaks of "art made tongue-tied by authority." Copyright was established by entry in the Stationers' Register, and (first things coming first) existed primarily for the benefit of the publisher rather than the author. The uncertain rewards of publication did not, however, discourage literary endeavor. Books of all sizes and shapes, from tiny duodecimos (their sheets folded into twelve leaves before being cut to produce twenty-four pages) to imposing folios (their sheets folded only once to yield two large leaves and four pages), issued from the presses.

On all subjects too: translations from the classical and modern European languages, chronicles of English history, etiquette and how-to-do-it manuals, school primers, poems erotic and heroical, sermons and devotional treatises, plays and prose fiction and satire. Amorous narrative poems on classical themes appealed to the lubricity of undergraduates, and early produced a masterpiece in Marlowe's *Hero and Leander.* Graver older readers were drawn to the pious tracts for which Eros proved no match: by the nineteenth century Lewis Bayly's *Practice of Piety* had gone through seventy-five editions. Formal verse satire, bilious or obscure (or as often both), enjoyed a vogue until the alarmed authorities in 1599 issued a restraining order and demanded copies of "such as had already given offense to be brought to the Bishop of London to be burnt." A landmark publication was the volume of the first three books of Edmund Spenser's *Faerie Queene* in 1590.

An advance of a different sort in the human condition was signaled by the appearance, in 1596, of Sir John Harington's *New Discourse of a Stale Subject, Called the Metamorphosis of Ajax,* describing the invention of the water closet. For this contribution Harington, as one physician has put it, "deserves to be held in memory by medical men as the inventor of the first apparatus in which the disposal of ordure by water carriage was controlled by mechanical means." There is some evidence that the Queen ordered a water closet, after Harington's design, to be installed in her palace at Richmond. But over two centuries were to go by before his innovation came into general use in England, reintroduced—and manufactured—by the ingenious Thomas Crapper.

Playbooks, often poorly printed, sold for sixpence on the stalls. On the whole the acting companies discouraged publication of their wares; once in print, plays could be performed by anybody. But plays did reach print for one reason or another: whether through theft or loss of vogue or the hard-pressed financial condition of the troupes. Along with the other varieties of literary expression, plays by his contemporaries furnished Shakespeare with source materials to sustain his endeavors for the troupe Polonius would have recognized as "the best actors in the world, either for tragedy, comedy, history, pastoral, pastoral-comical, historical-pastoral, tragical-historical, tragical-comical-historical-pastoral, scene individable, or poem unlimited." Elizabeth's London boasted no public libraries; in the bookstalls of St. Paul's, Shakespeare found his infinite riches in a little room.

A revolution, even one in which ink rather than blood flows, must exact a price. If the invention of printing made possible the cheap—or at least relatively inexpensive—duplication of books, it also rendered anachronistic the laboriously copied-out manuscripts that included among their number the illuminated treasures of the pre-Gutenberg world. Not that all calligraphers went on the dole. Professional scriveners like Ralph Crane found employment preparing presentation copies of poems by well-born amateurs or making fair copies of plays for actors. A handwriting manual of the period bears the title *The Pen's Excellency,* and that excellency was recognized. "To be brief," the author claims, "the art of writing is so excellent, and of such necessary use, that none ought to be without some knowledge therein, since the excellency of no art without it can be made known or manifest." One John Bale, "an Englishman born in the city of London," achieved celebrity with his microscopic calligraphy, one of his triumphs being a Bible snugly fitting into a walnut shell. Queen Elizabeth showed off to her ministers and resident ambassadors a specimen of Bale's handiwork mounted under crystal in a ring she wore. For his victory over rival penman Daniel Johnson in a public exhibition witnessed by a hundred, Bale was awarded a golden pen (more coveted than any latter-day senator's golden fleece), which thereafter

Below: *The interior of a sixteenth-century printing shop, showing two presses with compositors and proof-readers hard at work. This is the fourth in a series of twenty engravings from the drawings of Flemish artist Jan van der Straet illustrating the new technology and crafts of the sixteenth century. They were published by the Galle family during the 1580s at Antwerp under the title NOVA REPERTA.*

Opposite page: *Old St. Paul's Cathedral was a towering landmark in the city of* London. *In its churchyard many printers and booksellers had stalls to display and sell their wares. A small view of St. Paul's is provided in the diary of a German baron, Georg von Schwartzstät Freiherr von Offenbach, who visited England in 1609. Offenbach bought maps and prints, which he cut up and pasted in his diary as a pictorial record of his travels. This particular view is a vignette from John Speed's map of Middlesex, the county in which much of London is located.*

Below: *THE CANTERBURY TALES*, one of the most beautiful works from the press of England's first printer, William Caxton. Printed at Westminster around 1478, Caxton's edition followed the old manuscript tradition of "rubricating" (or rendering in red) the large ornamental initial letters. A small printed letter indicated to the rubricator the capital letter to be inked in by hand. Opposite page, top left: *HERO AND LEANDER* (London, 1598), the celebrated erotic narrative poem on a classical theme by Shakespeare's fellow dramatist Christopher Marlowe. This is the only copy of this edition known to have survived.

Center (top and bottom) and right center: *William Gilbert's work on the magnet, DE MAGNETE* (1600), was the first major scientific treatise to be written by an Englishman. Gilbert declared that the whole earth acted as a magnet. Other experiments described in his book qualify him as the first writer on electrical force.

Top far right: *Sir John Harington's invention of the water closet is graphically displayed in A NEW DISCOURSE OF A STALE SUBJECT, CALLED THE METAMORPHOSIS OF AJAX* (London, 1596). Ajax was a euphemism for jakes, the Elizabethan word for privy. Jakes is a form of the name Jack, a diminutive of John. Harington, a godson of Queen Elizabeth, had installed his water closet at his estate of Kelston near Bath. Unfortunately, the publication of his Rabelaisian book offended the Queen.

Bottom left: *The rare first issue of the first edition of Edmund Spenser's influential allegorical poem, THE FAERIE QUEENE* (London, 1590), the most notable achievement of Elizabethan non-dramatic verse.

Bottom right: *Specimen sheet of six typefaces thought to have been designed by the Flemish typefounder Francois Guyot and used by various printers on the Continent and in England between 1546 and 1700. Probably sent to a London printer who wanted to purchase type, it has manuscript price annotations. It has been dated as early as 1565, and is the only surviving copy of the earliest specimen sheet known to exist.*

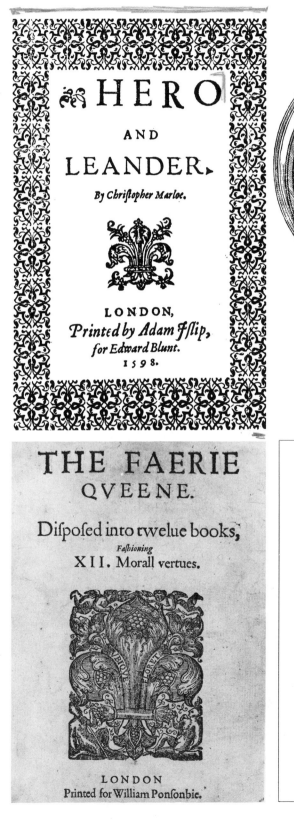

HERO
AND
LEANDER.

By Christopher Marloe.

LONDON,
Printed by Adam Iſlip,
for Edward Blunt.
1598.

THE FAERIE
QVEENE.

Diſpoſed into twelue books,
Faſhioning
XII. Morall vertues.

LONDON
Printed for William Ponſonbie.

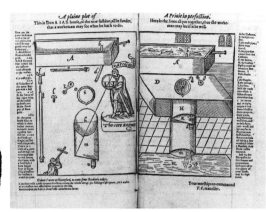

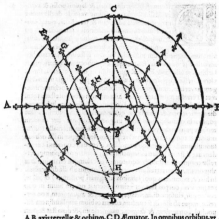

DE MAGNETE, LIB. III.   139

CAP. XII.

Quomodò verticitas exiſtit in ferro quouis excoĉto
magnete non excito.

Actenùs naturales & ingenitas cauſas, & acquiſitas per lapidem potentias declarauimus: Nunc verò & in excoĉto ferro lapide non excito, magneticarum virtutum cauſæ rimandæ ſunt. Admirabiles nobis magnes & ferrum promunt & oſtendunt ſubtilitates. Demonſtratum eſt anteà ſæpiùs, ferrum lapide non excitum in ſeptentiones ferri & meridiem; ſed & habere verticitatem, id eſt proprias & ſingulares polares diſtinĉtiones, quemadmodùm magnes, aut ferrum magnete attritum. Iſtud quidem mirum & incredibile primùm videbatur: Ferri metallum ex vena in fornace excoquitur, effluit ex fornace, & in magnâ maſſam indureſcit, maſſa illa diuiditur in magnis officinis, & in bacilla ferrea extenditur, ex quibus fabri rurſus plurima componunt inſtrumenta, & ferramenta neceſſaria. Ita variè elaborata & in plurimas ſimilitudines eadem maſſa transformatur. Quid eſt igitur illud quod

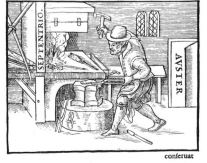

conſeruat

206   GVILIEL. GILBERTI.

diſponunt magnetica, & incitant, ac ſi orbes virtutum ſolidi eſſent & materiati magnetes: non enim per omne medium procedit, & vt in corpore continuo realiter exiſtit magnetica vis: ita orbes ſunt magnetici, & tamen non orbes reales nec per ſe exiſtentes.

Diagramma motuum in orbibus magneticis.

A B axis terrellæ & orbium, C D Æquator. In omnibus orbibus, vt in terrella, in æquatore verſorium ad Horizontis planum componitur; in axe vbique perpendiculariter centrum reſpicit; in medijs interuallis E reſpicit D, & G reſpicit H, non F, quod L verſorium in ſuperficie terrellæ reſpicit. Sed qualis eſt proportio L ad F in ſuperficie terrellæ, talis eſt G ad H in ſuo orbe, & E ad D in orbe ſuo; tales

M.M.N.N.O.P.Qu.R.S.T.V.X.Y.Z
A.a.b.c.d.e.f.g.h.i.k.l.m.n.o.p.q.r.ſs.t.v.v.u.w.
x.y.z.&.ff.ſſ.ß.ſt.ſi.ſi.fl.ſl.ſp.ſt.ĉt.ll.æ.œ.as.is.us. j
ij.ra.ta.ç.ĝ.ĝ.q̃.ã.ẽ.ĩ.õ.ũ.á.à.â.ẽ.é.è.ê.ẽ.í.ì.î.ĩ.ó.ò.ô.ú
.ú.û.:.-.,.(.:.!.;.'.'.a.e.m.n

Ϳn principio erat verbum, & verbum erat apud.&c
Amen dico vobis, ego ſum vitis vera, & pater meus
agricola eſt. Omnem palmitem in me non ferentem
fruĉtum, tollit: & omnem qui fert fruĉtum, purgat:
vt copioſiorem fruĉtum afferat. Manete in me, &
ego in vobis. Iam vos mundi eſtis propter ſermonem
quem loquutus ſum vobis. & reliqua. ibidem.

Above: *Esther Inglis's ARGUMENTA PSALMORUM was a New Year's gift to Henry, Prince of Wales and son of James I, in 1608. The preliminary leaves of this book contain a Latin dedication to the prince and a rendering of his coat of arms.*
Center and bottom: *Pages from OCTONARIES UPON THE VANITIE AND INCONSTANCIE OF THE WORLD, a manuscript dating from 1607 by Esther Inglis, "matchless mistress of the golden pen." It contains fifty stanzas of eight lines each, penned in different calligraphic styles and illustrated with flowers or fruit at the top of each right-hand page.*

became the sign over his door in Paul's Churchyard.

Esther Inglis was not English but French (her name is an anglicized version of Langlois), having been brought to London by refugees from the Bartholomew Day massacre of 1572. Her mother, Marie Prissott, taught her calligraphy. Inglis's meticulously executed little manuscript volumes, some illustrated with painted flowers, attracted as patrons Queen Elizabeth and the royal family of Scotland. James VI, who would become James I of England, appointed her nurse to Henry, Prince of Wales.

In this period the Italian hand, product of Renaissance Humanism and precursor of our own cursive script, gradually encroached upon the domain of the most favored English hand, called secretary because it was the usual secretary's hand and was generally used for the "dispatching of all manner of businesses for the most part whatsoever." The upper classes saw to it that their children mastered the Italian, more elegant and legible than secretary; but a glover's son like Shakespeare, educated in a provincial grammar school, would have learned secretary. So the six surviving signatures he affixed to legal documents attest. The courts and government departments developed their own specialized scripts.

Below: *English needlework bindings from the early part of the seventeenth century. Mostly in crewel or petit-point (or in combinations of the two), the designs, mainly floral, are worked on satin or canvas backgrounds. The volumes are small Bibles, New Testaments, and Psalms used by ladies.*

The English secretary alphabet (used by Shakespeare) and the small letters of the Italian or Latin hand are shown in this 1611 edition of Jean de Beauchesne and John Baildon's NEW BOOKE CONTAINING ALL SORTS OF HANDS (first published as DIVERS SORTES OF HANDS, ca. 1570). This copy once belonged to Elizabethan herald Augustine Vincent (the earliest recorded owner of a Shakespeare First Folio), and it has his coat of arms stamped on the vellum binding.
Below: "How you ought to hold your pen," a woodcut from the same book.

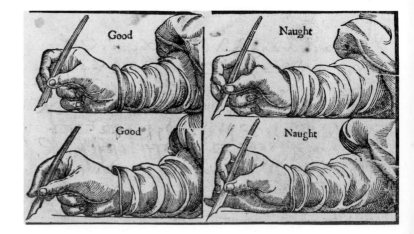

This page, above: *The first recorded purchase of Shakespeare's first printed book, VENUS AND ADONIS, is entered in the diary account book of Richard Stonley, June 12, 1593. Known in the eighteenth century, Stonley's diaries disappeared from view for almost 200 years. They came to light again when they were purchased by the Folger in 1972.*
Below: *VENUS AND ADONIS, Shakespeare's first published work, is shown here in the only known copy of an edition printed about 1595. All early editions of the poem, first published in 1593, are extremely rare.*

June 1593 9

Die Lune 11 Junij Barnabe apostle

Cato Despice divitias si vis animo esse beatus
Quas qui suspiciunt mendicant semper avari

Die Martis 12 Junij

Cato Commoda naturae nullo tibi tempore deerunt
Si contentus eo fueris quod postulat usus

VENVS AND ADONIS.

An Ouen that is ſtopt, or riuer ſtayd,
Burneth more hotly, ſwelleth with more rage:
So of concealed ſorow may be ſayd,
Free vent of words loues fier doth aſſwage,
But when the hearts atturney once is mute,
The client breakes, as deſperat in his ſute.

He ſees her comming, and begins to glow,
Euen as a dying coale reuiues with winde,
And with his bonnet hides his angrie brow,
Lookes on the dull earth with diſturbed minde:
Taking no notice that ſhe is ſo nye,
For all askance he holds her in his eye.

O what a ſight it was wiſtly to view,
How ſhe came ſtealing to the wayward boy,
To note the fighting conflict of her hew,
How white and red, each other did deſtroy:
But now her cheeke was pale, and by and by
It flaſht forth fire, as lightning from the skie.

Now was ſhe iuſt before him as he ſat,
And like a lowly louer downe ſhe kneeles,
With one faire hand ſhe heaueth vp his hat,
Her other tender hand his faire cheeke feeles:
His tender cheeke, receiues her ſoft hands prin
As apt as new falne ſnow, takes any dint.
B ij

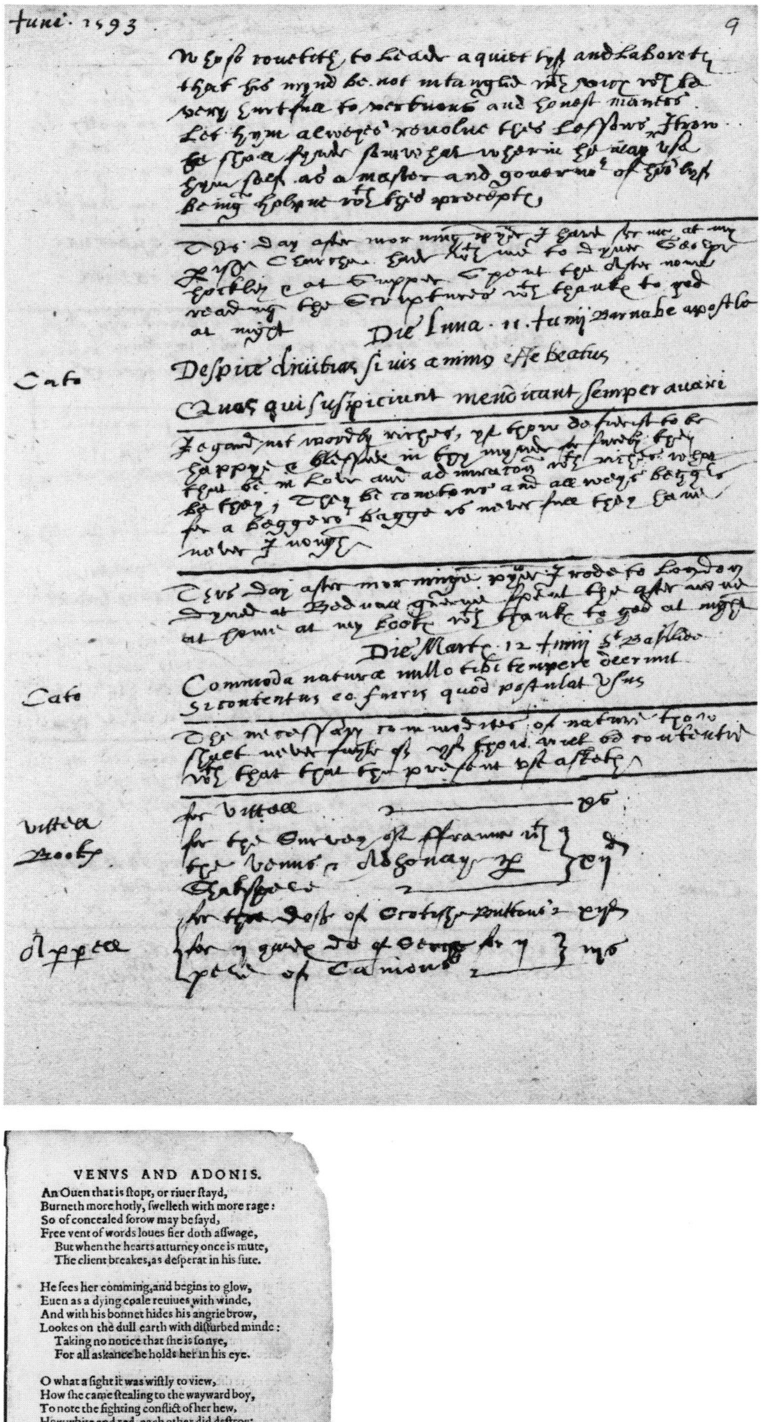

Secretary was presumably the script in which Shakespeare composed *Venus and Adonis,* his long erotic narrative poem in the manner of Marlowe's *Hero and Leander.* A fellow townsman, Richard Field, who ran a thriving establishment in the Blackfriars, printed *Venus and Adonis,* with unusual care—there are few misprints—in 1593. (Field also set Beauchesne and Baildon's *Book Containing Divers Sorts of Hands.*) Shakespeare's name does not appear on the title page of the first quarto edition of this poem, but the dedication of his "unpolished lines" to Henry Wriothesley, Earl of Southampton, is subscribed "Your Honor's in all duty, William Shakespeare." He had, then, found a noble patron.

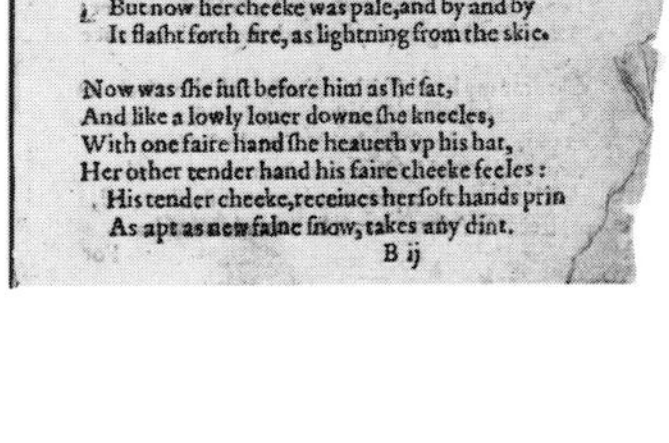

He also found a customer who left a curious record of that fact. On June 12, 1593, Richard Stonley, an elderly civil servant (one of the four tellers of the Exchequer), noticed a copy of *Venus and Adonis* on John Harrison's bookstall at the sign of the White Greyhound in Paul's Churchyard. Stonley laid out sixpence for the poem, and duly recorded his extravagance, along with another outlay of sixpence for Eliot's *Survey, or Topographical Description of France,* in his Diary Account Book. In so doing, Stonley became the first recorded purchaser of Shakespeare's first book.

There cannot have been very many customers crowding Paul's Churchyard that June day. For the bubonic plague gripped London. In the unsanitary tenements and hovels, in the goods-laden shops and fetid Town Ditch, the black rat thrived, carrying the flea that transmitted the plague bacillus. Eventually the brown rat, not a carrier, would win out over the black in the struggle for survival; but that was not for many years to come. Meanwhile, in a single year, from December 1592 until December 1593, almost eleven thousand souls perished. During these terrible times the street cry "Bring out your dead" echoed through the city as carts laden with corpses rumbled by. Those who could afford to flee to the purer air of the country did so. Among them were many doctors; the capital was desperately short of the medical services which might, perhaps, have saved some lives. Because they attracted large numbers of people, public playhouses were regarded as likely sources of infection and were wholesomely shut down by the municipal authorities. Churches, on the other hand, remained open. The players fell on hard times. They sought to eke out a living by going off on extended provincial tours; some even went into the Low Countries. When they returned, they sometimes found their families wiped out by disease.

Some biographers speculate that during the two-year onslaught of plague Shakespeare traveled in Italy, where he acquired the knowledge of Italian topography and customs displayed to such advantage in his subsequent plays. More likely, he stayed at home to write *Venus and Adonis* (with its Poor Wat and other bucolic reminiscences of the Warwickshire countryside) and *The Rape of Lucrece,* the "graver labor" promised in his first poem. *Lucrece* too he dedicated, with rather more warmth than his preceding effort, to the Earl of Southampton, whom he wished "long life still lengthened with all happiness." Shakespeare may also have written most of his sonnets during the plague years. But the complete sonnet cycle was not published until some time later, in 1609.

The two narrative poems found a receptive public. Sixteen editions of *Venus and Adonis* came off the presses before 1640. Few copies have escaped the jaws of devouring time, and those that have give every evidence of being well thumbed. *The Rape of Lucrece,* less spectacularly popular, achieved eight editions during the same period—a respectable number for a graver labor. Despite this success, however, Shakespeare made no further offerings to his dedicating muse. Perhaps the expected rewards failed to materialize; dedicatees, as a breed, were notoriously ungrateful. Whatever the external circumstances (and on these we can only speculate), Shakespeare's heart was clearly in the theatre. When, by spring 1594, the dangers of sickness had abated and the players once again trod the boards, he rejoined them.

For a brief time the Lord Chamberlain's Men acted in the Cross Keys Inn in Gracious Street, but before the year ended they had transferred to The Theatre, the house that James Burbage built. Burbage's son Richard would be the first to bring to theatrical life Shakespeare's great tragic parts: Richard III and (in the words of the actor's eulogist) "kind Lear, the grieved Moor, and more beside, / That lived in him." For the balance of his remarkably stable professional career Shakespeare would remain identified with the same troupe. When they moved to the Globe on Bankside, he accompanied them. Later, in the reign of James I, after the Chamberlain's company had become the King's Men, Shakespeare stayed on. Presumably he went with them when they played at Court by royal command or acted before less sophisticated auditors on the provincial circuit. For almost two decades Shakespeare was his company's "ordinary poet"—that is, its principal regular dramatist—providing on average two new plays each season.

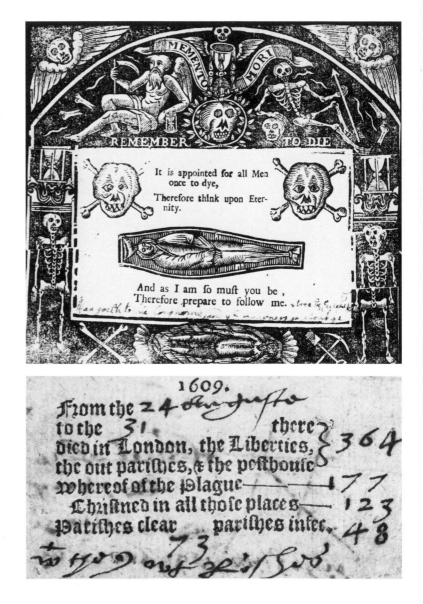

LVCRECE.

AN·CHORA·SPEI.

LONDON.

Printed by Richard Field, for Iohn Harrison, and are
to be sold at the signe of the white Greyhound
in Paules Churh yard. 1594.

To show me worthy of their sweet respect,
Then may I dare to boast how I doe loue thee,
Til then, not show my head where thou maist proue me

27

WEary with toyle, I hast me to my bed,
  The deare repose for lims with trauaill tired,
But then begins a iourny in my head
To worke my mind, when boddies work's expired.
For then my thoughts (from far where I abide)
Intend a zelous pilgrimage to thee,
And keepe my drooping eye-lids open wide,
Looking on darknes which the blind doe see.
Saue that my soules imaginary sight
Presents their shaddoe to my sightles view,
Which like a iewell (hunge in gastly night)
Makes blacke night beautious, and her old face new.
  Loe thus by day my lims, by night my mind,
  For thee, and for my selfe, noe quiet finde.

28

HOw can I then returne in happy plight
  That am debard the benifit of rest?
When daies oppression is not eazd by night,
But day by night and night by day oprest.
And each (though enimes to ethers raigne)
Doe in consent shake hands to torture me,
The one by toyle, the other to complaine
How far I toyle, still farther off from thee.
I tell the Day to please him thou art bright,
And do'st him grace when clouds doe blot the heauen:
So flatter I the swart complexiond night,
When sparkling stars twire not thou guil'st th' eauen.
  But day doth daily draw my sorrowes longer, (stronger
  And night doth nightly make greefes length seeme

29

WHen in disgrace with Fortune and mens eyes,
  I all alone beweepe my out-cast state,

And

An I trouble deafe heauen with my bootlesse cries,
And looke vpon my selfe and curse my fate.
Wishing me like to one more rich in hope,
Featur'd like him, like him with friends possest,
Desiring this mans art, and that mans skope,
With what I most inioy contented least,
Yet in these thoughts my selfe almost despising,
Haplye I thinke on thee, and then my state,
(Like to the Larke at breake of daye arising)
From sullen earth sings himns at Heauens gate,
  For thy sweet loue remembred such welth brings,
  That then I skorne to change my state with Kings.

30

WHen to the Sessions of sweet silent thought,
  I sommon vp remembrance of things past,
I sigh the lacke of many a thing I sought,
And with old woes new waile my deare times waste:
Then can I drowne an eye (vn-vs'd to flow)
For precious friends hid in deaths dateles night,
And weepe a fresh loues long since canceld woe,
And mone th'expence of many a vannisht sight.
Then can I greeue at greeuances fore-gon,
And heauily from woe to woe tell ore
The sad account of fore-bemoned mone,
Which I new pay, as if not payd before.
  But if the while I thinke on thee (deare friend)
  All losses are restord, and sorrowes end.

31

THy bosome is indeared with all hearts,
  Which I by lacking haue supposed dead,
And there raignes Loue and all Loues louing parts,
And all those friends which I thought buried.
How many a holy and obsequious teare
Hath deare religious loue stolne from mine eye,
As interest of the dead, which now appeare,
But things remou'd that hidden in there lie.

C 3   To

Opposite page: *Portrait of Shakespeare painted in oil on an oval wood panel. Derived from the Chandos portrait, it is thought to have been the shop sign of Jacob Tonson, prosperous London publisher, at his place of business, the Shakespeare's Head in the Strand, from 1710 to 1720.*
Top left: *The only known original copy of Shakespeare's first printed play, TITUS ANDRONICUS (London, 1594). After 1691, no copy was known to exist until 1904, when a postal clerk in Malmo, Sweden, discovered it among his family's possessions. The discovery was reported in the* New York Times *in January 1905, and Henry Folger imme-* diately dispatched his English agent to secure it. When found, the play was wrapped in an eighteenth-century lottery ticket, which has remained bound with it to the present day.*
Top right: *LOVES LABORS LOST (London, 1598), was Shakespeare's first comedy to be printed, and the first play in which his name appears on the title page.*
Bottom: *An early listing of Shakespeare's plays is given by Francis Meres, "Master of Artes of both Universities" (Oxford and Cambridge), in his PALLADIS TAMIA, WITS TREASURY (London, 1598).*

Popular plays at the box office: a measure of Shakespeare's success is that his plays were early to receive the undesired accolade of print. The first to appear in a quarto edition was *The Most Lamentable Tragedy of Titus Andronicus,* published in 1594 "As it was played by the Right Honorable the Earl of Derby, Earl of Pembroke, and Earl of Sussex their Servants." Evidently *Titus* had made the rounds in the pre-plague years before Shakespeare hitched his fortune to the Chamberlain's star. His name fails to appear on the title page. Nor does Shakespeare receive credit for *2 Henry VI,* pirated (the same year) almost unrecognizably as *The First Part of the Contention Betwixt the Two Famous Houses of York and Lancaster.* A villainously corrupt edition of *3 Henry VI* in the guise of *The True Tragedy of Richard, Duke of York* saw print, with discreet anonymity, in 1595. Two years later *Romeo and Juliet, Richard II,* and *Richard III* were published, also without attribution. Shakespeare's name occurs for the first time on the title page of a playbook in 1598—with *Love's Labor's Lost* and the second editions of *Richard II* and *Richard III.*

Whether or not Shakespeare was given title-page credit for his plays, before the end of the century enthusiasts of the stage had become aware of the prodigy in their midst. So much we may gather from a publication of 1598: *Palladis Tamia, Wit's Treasury,* compiled by Francis Meres, an M.A. of the two universities and a student of divinity, who, settled into his Botolph Lane lodgings, kept abreast of the literary and theatrical currents eddying about him. As a patriotic Elizabethan, Meres endeavors to show by means of enumerated comparisons—similitudes, as he terms them—that English poets, painters, and musicians can hold their own with the foreign competition. Thus it is that in his "Comparative discourse of our English poets, with the Greek, Latin, and Italian poets," Meres singles out Shakespeare. "As the soul of Euphorbus was thought to live in Pythagoras," Meres proclaims, "so the sweet witty soul of Ovid lives in mellifluous and honey-tongued Shakespeare; witness his *Venus and Adonis,* his *Lucrece,* his sugared Sonnets among his private friends, etc." The passage furnishes our earliest reference to Shakespeare's Sonnets, but even greater interest attaches to Meres's listing of the plays:

> As Plautus and Seneca are accounted the best for comedy and tragedy among the Latins, so Shakespeare among the English is the most excellent in both kinds for the stage. For comedy, witness his *Gentlemen of Verona,* his *Errors,* his *Love Labor's Lost,* his *Love Labor's Won,* his *Midsummer's Night Dream,* and his *Merchant of Venice;* for tragedy, his *Richard the Second, Richard the Third, Henry the Fourth, King John, Titus Andronicus,* and his *Romeo and Juliet.*

Falstaff, then, had made his debut by 1598, doing his part to increase the world's store of merriment, a commodity every age finds in chronically short supply. But what of *Love's Labor's Won*? No play of that name has come down, and simple error on Meres's part is ruled out by the fact that the same title appears independently in a stationer's stock-list drawn up in 1603. Does Meres refer to a lost Shakespeare comedy? The possibility that he might, and that, after four centuries, a copy could someday conceivably surface, is such stuff as Bardolaters' dreams are made on. More likely, *Love's Labor's Won* is an alternative title for an extant play. *Much Ado About Nothing* qualifies as a candidate. But so do some of Shakespeare's other romantic comedies, which tend generally to end with love's labors won. The *Palladis Tamia* entry turns out, then, to be a Meres nest.

In the same year a serious crisis faced Shakespeare's company. Their lease on The Theatre had run out, and by 1598 negotiations with the landlord, Giles Allen, broke down. He was prepared now to pull down the house and "convert the wood and timber thereof to some better use"—the puritanical implication being that planks could be better employed than to facilitate the staging of a *Romeo and Juliet* or a *Midsummer Night's Dream*. But Allen did not catch the Chamberlain's Men napping. They kept awake through the long night of December 28, 1598, to dismantle The Theatre (as their lease expressly allowed) and transport the timber across the Thames to Bankside. As they shrewdly assessed, this was the coming center for theatrical activity: Philip Henslowe, the age's leading theatrical entrepreneur, had built his Rose playhouse there in 1587, and Francis Langley, a buccaneer capitalist, the Swan in 1595. These were now joined by a new playhouse which for succeeding generations would be synonymous with Shakespeare's "wooden O": the Globe theatre, with its sign of Hercules bearing the world on his shoulders. By the end of 1599 it had opened its doors to the public. A foreign visitor, Thomas Platter of Basel, in that year reported seeing "the tragedy of the first Emperor Julius Caesar very pleasantly performed" on Bankside. His is the first reference to Shakespeare's *Julius Caesar* on the boards.

Although they tease rather than satisfy curiosity, the London panoramas give us an inkling of what the Globe (and other Bankside amphitheatres) looked like from the outside. Visscher shows a polygonal—probably hexagonal—structure, very similar to the Bear Garden just a little distance away. A draftsman of superior accomplishment, Hollar unhappily blundered by transposing the labels for the Globe and the Bear Garden: in his view the playhouse, shown in more convincing detail than in Visscher's view, is round. But then, in 1647, when Hollar published his panorama, the original Globe had long since vanished. In June 1613, during the first performance of Shakespeare's *Henry VIII,* the playhouse had burned to the ground when a spark from a stage cannon alighted in the thatched roof. The next year a second Globe, prudently roofed with tile, rose on the identical spot. This is the Globe that Hollar depicts. Was the original similarly round, or do we do better to trust Visscher? Such a question admits of no definite answer, for Visscher's panorama —our most familiar representation of London before the Great Fire of 1666—has numerous inaccuracies. Even his Thames is improbably straight. He may never have set foot in the capital; he may have simply trusted to conveniently available maps and views. Possibly he even confused the Globe with the nearby Rose, which is missing from his panorama.

Be that as it may, these early views bridge the centuries to give us a unique sense of the Shakespearean playhouse in its topographical setting. We see the surrounding shrubbery and tenements; we see the competing arena in which chained and blinded bears were tormented by hungry dogs for the amusement of holidaymakers; and, in the near distance, we see the silver-gliding Thames. The London theatres, each with an estimated capacity of some 3,000 spectators, were among the principal attractions of the metropolis for foreign visitors—much as the West End is for tourists today.

The Elizabethan theatre industry thrived on competition. Even before Shakespeare established himself as the monarch of the stage, it was already well on its way to establishing a

Top: *A close-up of Southwark and the Globe playhouse from Wenceslaus Hollar's long view of London (1647). The labels of the Bear-Baiting and Globe arenas have inadvertently been reversed.*
Bottom left: *Enlarged detail of Globe playhouse on the south bank of the Thames from Claes Jansz Visscher's long view of London, LONDINUM FLORENTISSIMA BRITANNIAE URBS (ca. 1625).*
Bottom right: *The Globe (mislabeled the Bear-Baiting arena) as shown in Hollar's long view of London (1647).*

Opposite page, above: *THE SPANISH TRAGEDIE, title page of an edition published in London in 1615. First printed ca. 1592, Thomas Kyd's play was a popular success and was reprinted many times. It anticipates HAMLET with its ghost, mad scenes, and theme of revenge. This is one of the earliest printings of a play in which a woodcut scene is used to illustrate the title page.*
Opposite page, below: *Title page of Christopher Marlowe's TRAGICALL HISTORIE OF THE LIFE AND DEATH OF DOCTOR FAUSTUS (London, 1631), with a woodcut depicting Faustus at his magical practices (shown, enlarged, on this page). Although Marlowe died in 1593, the first edition of this play did not appear until 1604.*

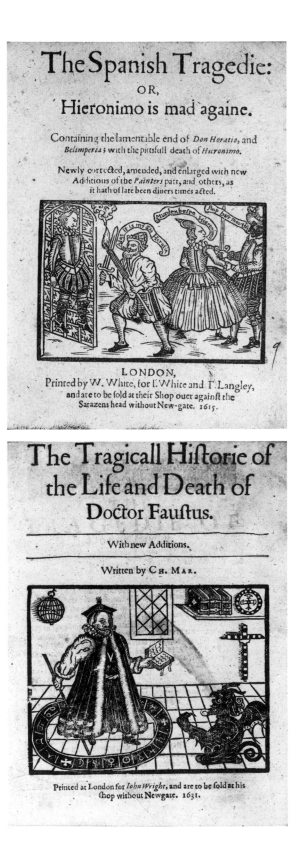

repertory of popular favorites. Christopher Marlowe, born in the same year as Shakespeare, enjoyed the advantage of an earlier start than his Stratford rival. With his conquering Tamburlaine, the Scythian shepherd who threatened the world with high astounding terms, Marlowe conquered popular audiences. He went on to achieve a mythic resonance with his Doctor Faustus, the savant who signs away his soul to Mephistophilis for "a world of profit and delight,/Of power, of honor, of omnipotence." That world is not without end, of course, but of twenty-four years' duration. Faustus pays the price of despair and damnation. As the clock strikes his final midnight and devils rush in to claim him, he cries, too late, "I'll burn my books!" Marlowe himself died violently at the age of twenty-nine. On May 30, 1593, the mighty line was extinguished at Dame Eleanor Bull's house in Deptford, not far from London. Scandalized contemporaries spread dark reports of Marlowe's blasphemies and atheism. But few secular plays are more suffused with religious consciousness than *Doctor Faustus.*

Another palpable hit, *The Spanish Tragedy* by Thomas Kyd (who once shared lodgings with Marlowe), went through ten editions in the period. Not one mentions the author; clearly the play was the thing. This one did much to establish a vogue for revenge drama. Audiences thrilled especially to the scene in which Horatio is murdered as he makes love to Bel-Imperia at nightfall in his father's pleasant bower. His assailants hang him from a tree, then spirit away the girl. For a few moments the stage remains bare—except for the dangling corpse. Then Horatio's father enters in his nightshirt. "What outcries pluck me from my naked bed," Hieronimo asks,

> And chill my throbbing heart with trembling fear,
> Which never danger yet could daunt before?
> Who calls Hieronimo?

Little wonder that this wonderfully constructed scene, with its astonishing range of emotion and tempo—its sudden explosion of violence, followed by poignant confrontation—made such a powerful impact on spectators. They had never seen the like before on the stage. Inevitably *The Spanish Tragedy* invited caricature—the tribute, as Oscar Wilde once put it, that mediocrity pays to genius—but it also served as the worthy forerunner of an infinitely more complex Elizabethan revenge play, Shakespeare's *Hamlet.*

An early sightseer, Johannes De Witt—a university student at Leyden who visited in 1596 or thereabouts—commented in his diary on the "notable beauty" of the London amphitheatres, and included a sketch of one. The Globe, of course, had not yet been built, but the Swan, which he drew, probably had essentially the same features. De Witt's diary has perished, but his fellow-student and friend Arend van Buchell was sufficiently impressed to copy the notes and sketch in his own commonplace book, which is preserved in the University Library at Utrecht. Otherwise, authentic pictorial material is scarce. What there is is supplemented by the contract for the Fortune theatre, which Henslowe built in 1600 as a rival to the Globe, employing the same carpenter, Peter Smith. The Fortune contract called for a square playhouse but in other respects aped the competition. Although the contract contains no plan, it conveniently furnishes the specifications for the Fortune. Apart from these scant resources, the student seeking to reconstruct the Elizabethan playhouse must depend mainly on the texts of the plays themselves—a task as challenging and as fraught with perplexity as any archaeological excavation of ancient remains.

Certain facts emerge, however, with reasonable clarity. Whether circular or polygonal, the amphitheatres were made of frame and plaster over a brick and pile foundation. Except for thatching over the galleries, they were unroofed, and thus open to the elements. Propped up by stout wooden trestles, the large rectangular stage—maybe forty feet across—jutted into the yard. At the back of this stage two massive doors in the facade of the tiring-house (the players' dressing room) allowed the actors to make their exits and entrances. A doorway, when curtained, could serve for a "discovery-space," such as that required for the concealment of Polonius in *Hamlet* or for the revelation of Hermione as a statue in *The Winter's Tale.* The upper story of the facade concealed the music room and did duty as a supplementary acting area—functioning as Juliet's balcony, for example, or as the rampart of a walled town, as in the siege of Harfleur in *Henry V.* At other times, in keeping with the economy of show business, this facility furnished additional space for paying customers. In the front of the thrust stage a trap door was available for the descent of the Ghost in *Hamlet* or for the burial of Ophelia. Rushes strewed the stage. Two pillars supported the "heavens," which extended to the rear facade. This cover furnished the actors with a shelter from the rain (spectators took their chances), and permitted the lowering of machinery required by the spectacular stagecraft of some plays. At the Globe the "heavens" were ornamented in keeping with the cosmological symbolism implicit in the playhouse name, expressive of Jaques's truism in *As You Like It* that "All the world's a stage." For the original audience, Hamlet's confession to Rosencrantz

and Guildenstern must have had a special *frisson:*

> this most excellent canopy the air, look you, this brave o'erhanging firmament, this majestical roof fretted with golden fire—why, it appeareth no other thing to me than a foul and pestilent congregation of vapours.

Above the "heavens" was a hut, or attic loft, from which the stagehands controlled the suspension gear for flying effects, such as the descent of Jupiter in *Cymbeline.* Perched on a platform attached to the roof of the hut, a trumpeter announced the commencement of each day's performance. Above flew a flag with the sign of the Globe.

At one or the other of the entrances, spectators gained admission to the yard for a penny. The yard offered standing room only. Three tiers of galleries stretched round the circumference of the playhouse. Here one might sit or stand for an additional penny. A superior place, usually high up, cost a third penny. The truly choice locations were in the lord's rooms partitioned off from the tiers closest to the stage. Performances took place during the day. Torches such as those used throughout *Macbeth,* or the light carried by Othello upon entering to find Desdemona asleep in her bed, sufficed to indicate a night scene.

Properties were sparely deployed: a table, a tree, a bed thrust out upon the stage would do when the imagination was willing. Shakespeare's great competitor Ben Jonson might sneer at how in the *Henry VI* plays the actors dared

> with three rusty swords,
> And help of some few foot and half-foot words,
> Fight over York and Lancaster's long jars,
> And in the tiring-house bring wounds to scars.

But our own stage has demonstrated how effective well-choreographed battle scenes can be with a handful of actors. Devoid of a proscenium arch and of movable scenery, the Elizabethan playhouse nevertheless achieved its miracles. Not that the dramatists were unmindful of their constraints. "Pardon, gentles all," begs the opening Chorus of *Henry V,*

> The flat unraised spirits that hath dar'd
> On this unworthy scaffold to bring forth
> So great an object. Can this cockpit hold
> The vasty fields of France? Or may we cram
> Within this wooden O the very casques
> That did affright the air at Agincourt?

*One of the earliest printed views of an
English stage performance is shown in
this frontispiece vignette to William
Alabaster's ROXANA TRAGAEDIA
(London, 1632).*

A view of an English stage just after the Restoration of Charles II, as presented in the engraved frontispiece to THE WITS, OR SPORT UPON SPORT (London, 1662), attributed to Francis Kirkman. The text consists of a medley of theatrical extracts, including several from Shakespeare.

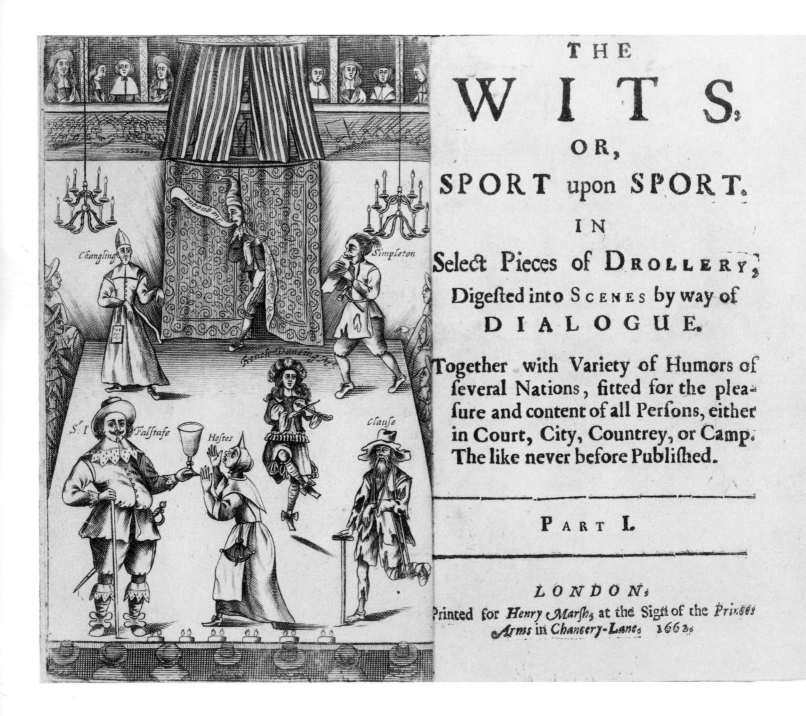

THE
WITS,
OR,
SPORT upon SPORT.
IN
Select Pieces of DROLLERY,
Digested into SCENES by way of
DIALOGUE.

Together with Variety of Humors of several Nations, fitted for the pleasure and content of all Persons, either in Court, City, Countrey, or Camp. The like never before Published.

PART I.

LONDON,
Printed for *Henry Marsh,* at the Sign of the *Princes Arms* in Chancery-Lane, 1662.

The answer, confirmed by a history of stage production that extends from Richard Burbage and the Chamberlain's Men to Alan Howard and the Royal Shakespeare Company, is a resounding yes.

At the Globe, geography presented no problem. The action of *Antony and Cleopatra* shuttles back and forth between Egypt and Rome; *Othello* moves effortlessly from Venice to Cyprus; *Pericles* traverses the coastal lands of the Aegean and eastern Mediterranean. Such limitations as the Elizabethan playwrights endured may actually have proved liberating. Language, not machines; the poet's art, not the scene-designer's—these created atmosphere. "I am fire and air," Cleopatra exults in her final transfiguration; "my other elements / I give to baser life." So, too, do we become fire and air with her. Machines and stage-designs, however sophisticated, are after all ephemeral. Only the imagination achieves endless monuments. Shakespeare knew as much when, in his eternizing sonnets, he proclaimed the power of his verse to live after "tyrants' crests and tombs of brass are spent." The architecture of the Elizabethan playhouse acknowledged the primacy of the word. And the word was the glory of the English Renaissance.

A pretty story relates how Queen Elizabeth, being "a great admirer of the immortal Shakespeare," often attended the theatre to see his plays. She is reported to have sat upon the stage or behind the scenes while he performed, on one occasion even dropping a glove, which he graciously stooped to retrieve for her. Like other pretty stories clustering around the memory of great men, this one merely rationalizes fantasy. For although the public playhouses attracted a broad spectrum of the population, from courtier to apprentice, royalty resisted queuing up for admittance. Yet the Queen did see Shakespeare's plays acted. That was when the Lord Chamberlain's Men were summoned to Richmond or Greenwich or Whitehall—wherever Elizabeth kept her Court—to participate in the festivities of the Christmas season. Thus did the grammar-school product in whose veins no blue blood coursed stray into the vestibule of power; thus did he catch glimpses of that world of intrigue and pomp which, as his history plays testify, he came to understand so well.

Over that world Elizabeth held sway as supreme potentate. The daughter of an anointed King, she was crowned at Westminster. Like her father, she ruled by divine right. She was also Supreme Governor of the Church of England: at every divine service the priest led prayers for her. Shakespeare makes the christening of Elizabeth the ecstatic finale of his *Henry VIII.* With a poet's leeway for prophetic hindsight, he has the Archbishop of Canterbury foretell her future greatness:

> She shall be lov'd and fear'd. Her own shall bless her:
> Her foes shake like a field of beaten corn,
> And hang their heads with sorrow. Good grows with her;
> In her days every man shall eat in safety
> Under his own vine what he plants, and sing
> The merry songs of peace to all his neighbours.
> God shall be truly known; and those about her
> From her shall read the perfect ways of honour,
> And by those claim their greatness, not by blood.

"She is our God in earth," said Lord North, unwilling to let the Bishop of Ely forget; and "if there be perfection in flesh and blood, undoubtedly it is in Her Majesty." Long after her teeth had turned black and a wig covered her faded hair, poets continued to extol the beauty of the divine Gloriana. When young, she had her father's red hair; and she was, like him, vain and imperious. She swore, picked her teeth, and—on occasion—boxed her counselors' ears. But she could also be exceedingly affable. As an admirer who knew her well observed, "The Queen did fish for men's souls, and had so sweet a bait that no one could escape her network."

She played the virginals, danced six or seven galliards a morning, and enjoyed chess. Unlike her father, she was abstemious when it came to food and drink. And sex. Henry married six times, but history would remember his daughter as the Virgin Queen.

Not that she lacked suitors, When they tickled her fancy, she tickled their necks. Of all her favorites, Lord Robert Dudley came closest to winning her. Proud and unprincipled, with a powerful aura of masculinity, he looked—and welcomed—the part of royal stud. "Lord Robert is the worst young fellow I have encountered," sighed the Spanish ambassador. "He is heartless, spiritless, treacherous and false." This was the Queen's "sweet Robin." She made him Master of the Horse, and later created him Baron of Denbigh and Earl of Leicester. When his wife died on a staircase by accident or suicide or murder (reports differed), Dudley was free to marry again, but not with Elizabeth. Such a match would only prove true the bitter mock of Elizabeth's cousin Mary Stuart: "The Queen of England is going to marry her horsekeeper who has killed his wife to make room for her."

No need; Elizabeth had other favorites to amuse her. There was Sir William Pickering, a diplomat, handsome, and a ladies' man, who entertained lavishly but affected dining apart "with music playing." Court bookmakers gave him a one-to-four chance in the royal matrimonial sweepstakes.

Another curled darling was Sir Christopher Hatton, of good Northamptonshire stock but no aristocrat (he had enrolled at Oxford as a gentleman–commoner). Arriving on the scene somewhat later, he impressed the Queen with his jousting and good parts. She rewarded him with dissolved monasteries, lands, and other rich presents, including a castle, and made him captain of her bodyguard. In the customary exchange of New Year's gifts between the monarch and her courtiers, Hatton regularly received four hundred ounces of silver plate, at least twice what most others were given. When Hatton fell grievously ill in 1573, Elizabeth visited him daily. Recovered, he wrote "Love me, for I love you," signing himself her "most happy bondman." She called him, affectionately, mutton. Eventually she appointed Hatton Lord Chancellor. When Sir Christopher died of diabetes on November 20, 1591, his funeral cortege included one hundred poor people furnished with caps and gowns for the occasion. They preceded the coffin, which was followed by four hundred gentlemen and yeomen, the lords of the council, and eighty gentlemen pensioners. Hatton's estate footed the bill for this state funeral; thus did the Queen combine splendor with parsimony. Despite the ostentation of his obsequies, and the inevitable rumor that he was the royal paramour, Hatton never rated as a matrimonial candidate. After all, he was a commoner.

Clemens et Regni moderatrix iusta Britani
Hac forma insigni conspicienda nitet.

Below: *A fanciful Elizabethan manuscript collection of verses honoring Queen Elizabeth in pictorial form. A small square of vellum when unfolded shows four figures resembling paper dolls, with foldover flaps at different heads and verses. There are eleven different mythological and Biblical figures; a twelfth is Queen Elizabeth herself. It is dated March 21, 1603 , a short time before the Queen's death.*

Above right: *Vellum roll signed by Queen Elizabeth listing the New Year's gifts given and received by her in 1563–64. The gifts include money, plate, jewelry, and items of costume exchanged between Elizabeth and the courtiers and state officials who served her.*

Middle right: *Queen Elizabeth's Bible. This large folio, bound in red velvet, once belonged to Queen Elizabeth and is decorated with silver clasps and bosses bearing her monogram, her coat of arms, and Tudor roses. It is a first issue of the 1568 revision known as the Bishops' Bible.*

Bottom right: *John Dowland's FIRST BOOKE OF SONGES OR AYRES (London, 1597) was written for four-part singing and printed so that when placed on a small table or stand it enabled each singer around the table to face his own part. Dowland also included tableture for accompaniment by the lute.*

Opposite page: *Coat of Arms of Queen Elizabeth I, early seventeenth-century illuminated drawing.*

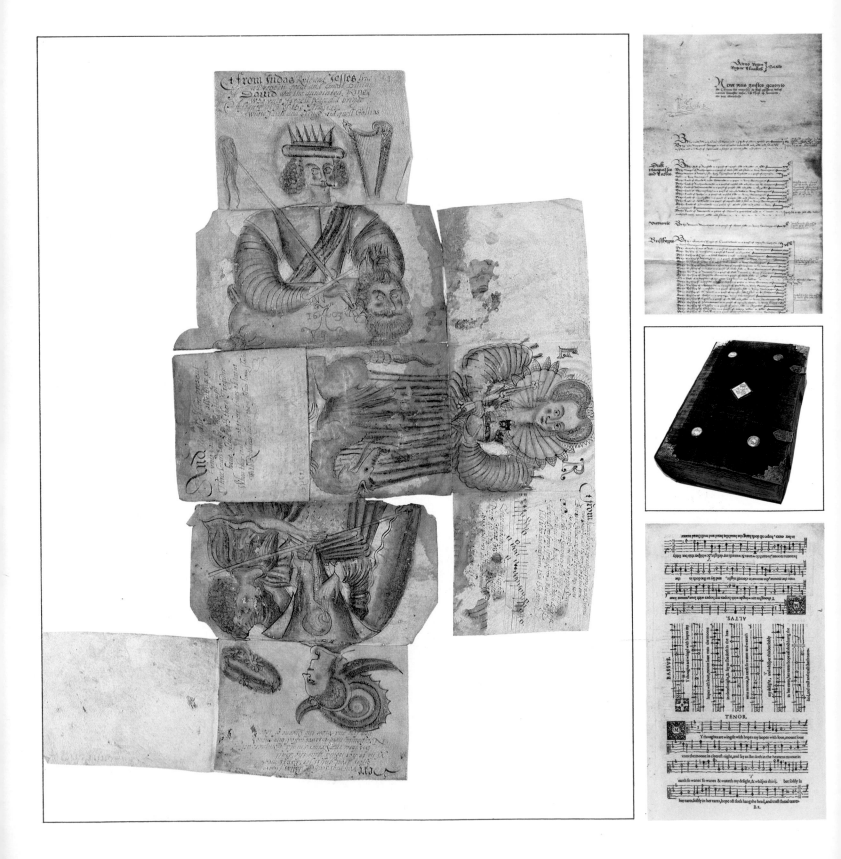

She had royals enough to choose from. For a decade Elizabeth dangled the Hapsburg Archduke Charles, who was presentable in a dignified sort of way and offered political advantages: on the one hand, alliance in the event that the Netherlands fell to Spain; on the other, no threat of merger with England, for he lacked a kingdom of his own. But from the outset, Elizabeth gave him little hope. "If I am to disclose to you what I should prefer if I follow the inclination of my nature," she declared, "it is this: Beggar-woman and single, far rather than Queen and married." Finally Charles took the hint and found matrimonial solace with a Bavarian princess.

France offered several possibilities. Catherine de Medici, herself somewhat *parvenu* in origin, touted her sons: first Charles IX, at fourteen neither enticing nor enticed; then the Duke of Anjou, eighteen to Elizabeth's thirty-seven. But he was unentranced by "an old hag with a sore leg," as he somewhat ungallantly described the Queen. Catherine's third son, the Duke of Alencon, wooed Elizabeth with some show of spirit, even though she was by then forty-five and he twenty years her junior. She found him handsome and called him her frog: he thus joined a select menagerie. But the prospect of a French connection stirred alarm among Elizabeth's subjects. John Stubbs injudiciously published a pamphlet, *The Discovery of a Gaping Gulf Whereinto England is Like to be Swallowed by Another French Marriage,* for which he was condemned to have his offending right hand cut off on the scaffold. This was done, whereupon Stubbs with his left hand lifted his hat from his head, shouted "God save the Queen," and fainted. Nothing came of Alencon's courtship, just as nothing had come of any of the others: Philip of Spain, Prince Eric of Sweden, the Duke of Holstein.

At the outset, Elizabeth had told her loyal Commons that she preferred maidenhood: "in the end, this shall be for me sufficient, that a marble stone shall declare that a Queen, having reigned such a time, lived and died a virgin." But few of her subjects took her at her word. Women, as the preachers declared, existed for marriage and childbearing. Besides, English monarchs, for whom procreation assumed an extraordinary importance, always (unless cut off young) found mates. In time Elizabeth's virginity, no less than her purported amours, spawned rumor. William Drummond of Hawthornden, a minor Scottish poet who played host to Ben Jonson, solemnly recorded the great man's assertion that the Queen "had a membrane on her, which made her uncapable of man, though for her delight she tried many. At the coming over of Monsieur [i.e., Alencon in 1579], there was a French surgeon who took in hand to cut it, yet fear stayed her, and his death."

HONI SOIT QVI MALY PENSE

SEMPER EADEM

Nata Gronewicie
anno Christi
MDXXXIII.
6. Id. Sept.

VERBVM
DEI

IVSTITIA

Opposite page: *Document on vellum issued February 5, 1561, under the name of Queen Elizabeth and granting highway rights to Sir Richard Lee. The Queen's great seal, molded in wax, is attached at the bottom, making it official.*
Below: *The obverse in wax of the first Great Seal of Queen Elizabeth I, showing the Queen enthroned, holding an orb and scepter.*

But causes weightier than the untimely demise of a surgeon impeded matrimony. Reasons of state militated against it. Had she chosen a husband from among the rivalrous, headstrong eligibles of her own court, Elizabeth would have upset the delicate balance of power, thus compromising her prerogatives of rule. Memories of dynastic struggles brought to a peaceful conclusion by the triumphal emergence of the Tudors were kept green by such works as the *Henry VI* plays and *Richard III.* England did not yearn for a reprise of the Wars of the Roses. On the other hand, if Elizabeth had looked abroad for a mate, she would have risked placing England under a foreign yoke: maybe a Catholic yoke at that, or a Calvinist one, in a Europe polarized by the legions of Reformation and Counter-Reformation. The role of politically neuter consort, for which Albert would in the fullness of time receive his Memorial, had not yet evolved. And meanwhile the disastrous consequences of Bloody Mary's marriage with Philip of Spain were still vividly recent. Whatever her personal inclinations, then, by remaining single but not discouraging hope, Elizabeth could exercise the checks and balances of power. As a canny Scottish ambassador (Scots in these anecdotes are always canny) told the Queen with permissible effrontery, "Ye think that if ye were married, ye would be but queen of England, and now ye are king and queen both. Ye may not suffer a commander." She would not and did not.

This truth was not yet self-evident when Elizabeth, a twenty-five-year-old girl with golden-red hair and exquisitely tapered hands, took over the reins of power in November 1558. As the best match in Europe, with the sceptered isle for her dowry, she could have her pick of husbands. And as Philip of Spain observed from afar, she was obliged to choose one to "relieve her of those labors which are only fit for men." Philip merely expressed the conventional wisdom which had lately been confirmed by the experiment with feminine rule under Mary. On the eve of Elizabeth's accession, the Scottish reformer John Knox sounded his *First Blast of the Trumpet Against the Monstrous Regiment of Women,* devoted to proving the proposition that "To promote a woman to bear rule, superiority, dominion or empire above any realm, nation, or city, is repugnant to nature, contumely to God, a thing most contrarious to His revealed will and approved ordinance, and finally it is the subversion of good order, of all equity and justice." Actually composed during Mary's last failing months, this tract is in Knox's best fire-eating style, and he promises "thrice to blow the trumpet in the same matter, if God so permit." But Elizabeth took the *Blast* as a personal insult, and Knox set down his trumpet.

He was the least of her worries, for she faced truly formidable odds. The world in which the Sovereign moved was overwhelmingly masculine. The courtiers who danced attendance upon her were men; so were the ministers over whom somehow she had to establish her authority. Even her trusted principal secretary, William Cecil, later created Lord Burghley, cautioned an ambassador's messenger about discussing with the Queen matters of "such weight" as were "too much for a woman's knowledge."

Yet Elizabeth would prove England's greatest monarch. How did she accomplish her triumph? Fortunately, despite her gender, she had received the education of a prince: an education expressive of the humanistic ideal of manifold accomplishment. The Italian courts of the Renaissance nourished that ideal, which, early in the century, found its most eloquent spokesman in Baldassare Castiglione. His *Il Cortegiano,* an imaginative record of conversations taking place on four successive spring evenings in 1507 at the Ducal Palace of Urbino, celebrates the complete man: scholar, soldier, athlete, connoisseur of the arts, arbiter of manners. The fourth dialogue, Bembo's Discourse, comprised (for the age) a definitive statement of the philosophy that exalted love to the status of Platonic vision. It is the downfall of the ideal that Ophelia laments when she describes the disheveled Hamlet:

O, what a noble mind is here o'erthrown!
The courtier's, soldier's, scholar's, eye, tongue, sword;
Th' expectancy and rose of the fair state,
The glass of fashion and the mould of form,
Th' observ'd of all observers—quite, quite down!

In Castiglione's dialogues women participate with the men as their social and intellectual equals. When Sir Thomas Hoby published his English translation in 1561, he addressed *The Courtier* to both sexes: the title page advertised the book as "Very necessary and profitable for young gentlemen and gentlewomen abiding in Court, Palace or Place." Never mind that manners at the Tudor court fell somewhat short of the ideal. As late as the next reign an English traveler on the Continent beheld forks for the first time. "This form of feeding I understand is generally used in all places of Italy," noted Thomas Coryat around 1608, "their forks being for the most part made of iron or steel, and some of silver, but those are used only by gentlemen. The reason of this their curiosity is, because the Italian cannot by any means endure to have his dish touched with fingers, seeing all men's fingers are not alike clean." Elizabeth managed with just a knife, and lifted her meat with her fingers. It is well to remember, however, that Castiglione himself glosses over the grossnesses of Urbino. The importance of such books as *The Courtier* lies not in their reflection of actuality but in their presentation of an image of the ideal.

To the achievement of that ideal Elizabeth's tutors made their contribution. Another Castiglione, Baptista, was her Italian master. An accomplished scholar, William Grindall, directed her classical studies. After Grindall's premature death in 1548, Roger Ascham became her tutor—a happy choice, and her own. Ascham helped to form Elizabeth's distinctive Italian hand. He supervised the mornings she gave to Greek and the afternoons she devoted to Latin. In his *Schoolmaster,* composed after Elizabeth had become Queen, Ascham affectionately recalls his aptest pupil: "Point forth six of the best given gentlemen of this court, and all they together show not so much good will, spend not so much time, bestow not so many hours daily, orderly, and constantly, for the increase of learning and knowledge, as doth the Queen's Majesty herself. Yea, I believe that beside her perfect readiness in Latin, Italian, French, and Spanish, she readeth here now at Windsor more Greek every day, than some prebendary of this church doth read Latin in a whole week."

The proficiency Elizabeth acquired served more than ornamental ends. None of the foreign ambassadors at her court spoke English, that language not yet having achieved diplomatic status; so she conversed with them in French or Italian—or in Latin, the universal language of the Renaissance. And she was able to supervise on her own—rather than delegate—vital, often extremely delicate, correspondence respecting negotiations of state. Besides, she loved conversation. When the French ambassador commended her mastery of languages as a great virtue in a princess, she twitted him, "It was no marvel to teach a woman to talk; it were far harder to teach her to hold her tongue."

Left: *THE COURTIER, by Baldassare Castiglione, was the most influential courtesy manual of the Renaissance. First published in Venice in 1528, it was translated into all the major European languages. This is the first English edition (London, 1561), translated by Thomas Hoby.*

Top right: *An early anti-feminist tract, THE FIRST BLAST OF THE TRUMPET AGAINST THE MONSTRUOUS REGIMENT OF WOMEN (Geneva, 1558), by the Scottish reformer John Knox. It was directed against three politically important women—Mary, Queen of Scots; her mother, Mary of Guise, Regent of Scotland; and Mary Tudor, Queen of England—all of whom opposed the Reformation.*

Bottom right: *Henry VIII's schoolbook, a copy of Cicero with commentary by Petrus Marus (Paris, 1502). In a large, bold hand, the young Prince of Wales wrote on the first leaf of text: "Thys boke is myne, Prynce Henry."*

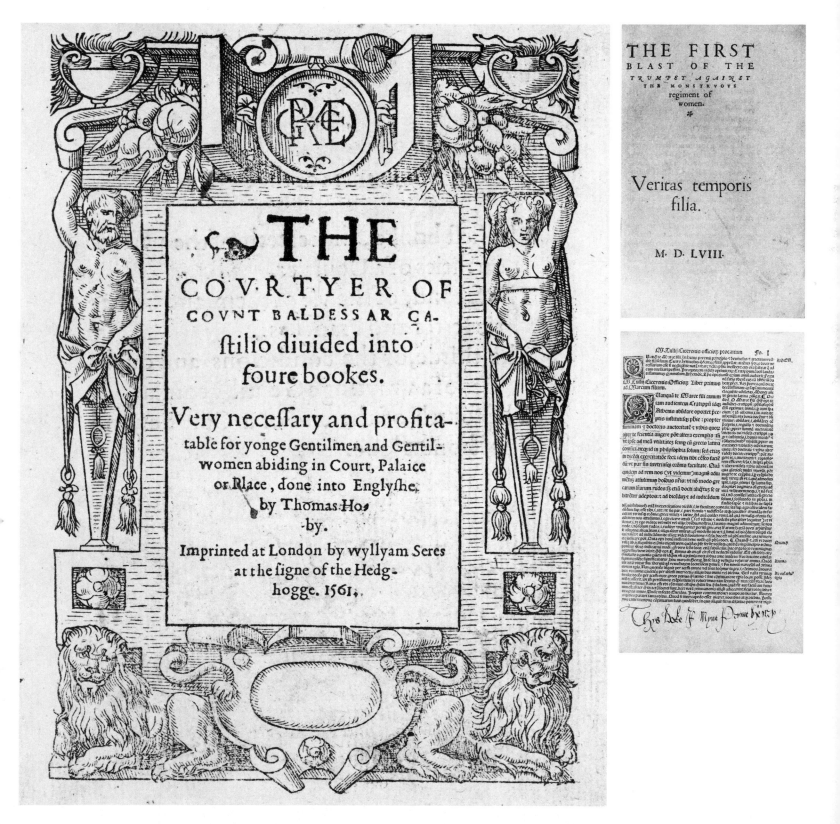

QUEEN ELIZABETH, *miniature oil painting after John de Critz, seventeenth-century.*

If, as the conventional wisdom here echoed alleged, she reveled in her loquacity as a female trait, she also used to advantage the other traditional attributes of her sex. She was vain and greedy of flattery. Each day saw her differently costumed, and when she died she left a wardrobe of perhaps two thousand dresses. In her finery, bedecked with jewels, Elizabeth played the coquette with her courtiers. By appealing to chivalric impulses which the Renaissance had not entirely displaced, she made herself the object of a cult of the virgin: the divine Gloriana. In his *Arraignment of Paris,* a pastoral performed before the Queen, George Peele plays a variation on ancient myth by having Diana, goddess of chastity, resign the Golden Apple to "fair Eliza," a decision applauded by the rival goddesses—Venus, Juno, and Pallas—who had competed for the prize.

> In state Queen Juno's peer, for power in arms
> And virtues of the mind Minerva's mate,
> As fair and lovely as the Queen of Love,
> As chaste as Dian in her chaste desires.
> The same is she, if Phoebe do no wrong,
> To whom this ball in merit doth belong.

Peele's flattery is shameless, but no more so than others'.

Shakespeare does this sort of thing more discreetly. For him allusion suffices. In *A Midsummer Night's Dream,* Oberon envisages the Virgin Queen as votaress of Diana, the moon goddess. He describes how once Cupid, all armed, took aim

> At a fair vestal, throned by the west,
> And loos'd his love-shaft smartly from his bow,
> As it should pierce a hundred thousand hearts;
> But I might see young Cupid's fiery shaft
> Quench'd in the chaste beams of the wat'ry moon;
> And the imperial vot'ress passed on,
> In maiden meditation, fancy-free.

Besides gratifying the imperatives of her own insatiable ego, the praises of Elizabeth—a chorus sustained for almost a half century—helped to fashion the special mystique that clung to her person. If ever a ruler had magnetism, it was she. And because she delighted in displaying herself to her subjects, Elizabeth became the most accessible of goddesses.

To these accomplishments, rooted in her sex, she added a Tudor toughness and practicality. A gifted administrator, she had a sharp eye for character, and made a series of brilliant appointments, of whom Cecil's was first and chief. Meanwhile, she reduced her Privy Council from a cumbersome forty-four to fewer than a score. Their advice she ignored when she chose. The Spanish ambassador, no stranger to the autocratic style, was impressed. This Queen, he reported to the Escorial, was "incomparably more feared than her sister"; she "gives her orders and has her way as absolutely as her father did." At the same time, Elizabeth knew the uses of tact. When she signed the first public document of her reign, she put an "etc." after her titles, whereas her father and brother before her had signed themselves Supreme Head of the Church. The "et cetera" was sufficient to assert the prerogative of the English Reformation, but sufficiently low-keyed to allow the Catholic world to hope.

Generally Elizabeth avoided extremes in politics and religion; statecraft was, for her, the art of the possible. Thus she evolved her characteristic style of governance, in which evasion and delay, agonizing reappraisal and last-minute retraction, became manifestations not of weakness but of the adroit exercise of policy. In this context the most dramatic moments of her reign assume, in their decisiveness, a paradoxical aspect. Elizabeth abhorred war, yet her age is memorable for England's greatest military triumph. She loathed having to reach decisions, yet she signed the death warrants for the cousin (Mary Stuart) and the erstwhile favorite (Essex) who had challenged her rule—although for the former she shifted responsibility by not herself ordering the warrant put into execution.

Mary Stuart's last curtain doubled as prologue to Philip II's Spanish tragedy. She had the Tudor golden-red hair, setting off big dark eyes and small cupid's-bow lips. She was a Catholic, and a Tudor on her father's side. Margaret, Henry VIII's sister, had married James IV of Scotland, a union which produced James V, who in turn married Mary of Guise. Of this match Mary Stuart was the sole surviving issue. Her father greeted the arrival, correctly, as a portent of disaster, and forthwith died. At the age of one week Mary became Queen of Scotland. In 1558, the year of her cousin Elizabeth's accession, she was yoked at fifteen, in matrimony with Francis, the Dauphin of France: a state rather than a love match. Within a year he was Francis II, and she the Queen of France. Another year, and he was dead; Mary found herself a teen-age Dowager Queen. This was not the same as being Queen in her own right, but were she to gain the crown of England—a prize many, including Mary, thought legitimately hers—she would possess a double kingdom. To achieve this devoutly-wished consummation, Mary connived, dissembled, and plotted with a persistence matched only by its ineptitude.

Her love-life hardly proved an asset. For her second husband she took Lord Darnley, the grandson (by a second marriage) of Mary's own grandmother Margaret Tudor. With his long slender legs, beardless girlish face, and close-cropped blond hair, Darnley, three years her junior, struck her as "the lustiest and best proportioned long man that she had seen." He was also stupid and arrogant, and a drunkard to boot. The marriage was in every respect a disaster: Elizabeth and her council worried that the Tudor alliance strengthened Mary's hand; the Scots were unhappy because Darnley was embroiled in ancient clan feuds; and once the novelty had worn off, Mary found herself saddled with an insufferable nincompoop. She found solace with her baseborn Italian secretary and former musician, David Riccio: Seigneur Davie, as the upstart was mockingly called. When Mary became pregnant, rumor held that she carried Seigneur Davie's child. Banished from his wife's bed, in March 1566 the unhappy Darnley conspired with the Protestant lords to eliminate Riccio. They burst in upon him as he sat at supper with the Queen at Holyrood House. Riccio literally hid behind Mary's skirts, but in vain. His assailants dragged him into an outer chamber and cut him down with fifty-six thrusts of sword and dagger. "No more tears," Mary reportedly said when informed of Riccio's death, "I will think upon a revenge."

Revenge came. First, however, she had to give birth. The story goes that when word of Mary's delivery was brought to Elizabeth, she cried to her ladies, "The Queen of Scotland is lighter of a fair son, and I am but a barren stock!" Being thus lighter, the Queen of Scotland took a new lover, the Earl of Bothwell, who won her affections macho style by raping her. She was ready for a masterful man even if he happened to be a Protestant. Then in 1567 she lured Darnley to a little house at Kirk o' Field, just outside Edinburgh. While she was away, having happily remembered a previous engagement, a violent explosion blew up the house. When the dust settled, Darnley's body was found in the neighboring garden—strangled, rumor had it. Although Bothwell was the prime suspect, Mary defiantly married him. She had now gone too far. The nobility rebelled, Bothwell fled, and Mary was carried prisoner to Edinburgh, where the crowds shouted "Burn the whore." She was imprisoned and forced to abdicate, but within less than a year she had escaped and raised an army of six thousand, which was decisively defeated at Langside, near Glasgow. Recapture would mean death for her. Mary fled across the border and threw herself on her cousin's mercy.

For almost twenty years she remained Elizabeth's unwelcome guest. Ungrateful, too, for that matter. She plotted and intrigued with followers at home and Catholics across the seas. A Florentine merchant-banker in London, Roberto di Ridolfi, enlisted the enthusiastic support of the Papacy and the Duke of Norfolk in a conspiracy to assassinate Elizabeth, free Mary, and restore the true faith to England. From her comfortable confinement at Chatsworth, Mary gave her blessing to the enterprise. But it backfired and Ridolfi hurried back to Italy, leaving Norfolk to face the executioner's axe. Parliament would gladly have seen Mary suffer a similar fate, but Elizabeth could not bring herself to order the execution of a woman, her cousin, and an anointed sovereign—not to mention her legal heir, and recognized by Elizabeth as such. So Mary was permitted to go on scheming for fifteen more years. The Babington Conspiracy, in 1586, was the last straw. It followed a familiar pattern. A small band—six in this case—would kill the Queen, while a foreign force invaded England. Mary would be rescued. Anthony Babington, once a page in the Earl of Shrewsbury's household, thought so well of the plot, of which he was a prime mover, that he hired an artist to make portraits of the conspirators "as a monument to so worthy an act." He also injudiciously described the plans in a letter to Mary, who—even more injudiciously—responded at length, clearly implying that she looked forward to the murder of Elizabeth, and even offering a few suggestions about how best to achieve that beneficent end. Elizabeth's secret service, under Sir Francis Walsingham, intercepted the correspondence. Mary was finished.

*Mary, Queen of Scots, and Henry
Stuart, Lord Darnley (her husband).
An engraving by Renold Elstrackæ,
probably dating from about 1603, the
year in which their son, James I, succeeded to the English throne.*

Are to be folde at Popes head Alley at the white horfe
by Iohn Sudbury and George Humble

R. Elftrak
ſculp

Letter from Queen Elizabeth to Philip II of Spain, dated February 17, 1565. Although signed by the Queen, it is written in Latin in the hand of her secretary, Roger Ascham. It requests the release of English merchants detained with their goods and ships in Spain.

At Fotheringay Castle in Northamptonshire, thirty-six commissioners tried Mary. She lied, denying knowledge of the conspiracy despite the overwhelming weight of evidence, including Babington's own testimony. Still Elizabeth hesitated to sign the death warrant; if only Mary would make a full confession and show sincere penitence. But she would not. "Full grievous is the way," Elizabeth lamented, "that I, who have in my time pardoned so many rebels, winked at so many treasons... should now be forced to this proceeding against such a person." Having finally signed the order, she cast it to the floor rather than handing it to her secretary; it was secretly conveyed to Fotheringay lest the Queen change her mind. There Mary Stuart, Queen of Scotland, was executed on February 8, 1587.

Mary was forty-four, dumpy, and round-shouldered. Her auburn hair was fake. As the Dean of Peterborough exhorted her to find salvation by changing her religion, she disdainfully interrupted: "Master Dean, I shall die as I have lived, in the true and holy Catholic faith. All you can say to me on that score is but vain, and all your prayers, I think, can avail me but little." On the platform, with its improvised block, in the Great Hall, she held high the crucifix and prayed for England and her royal cousin Elizabeth. She forgave her enemies. Then Mary of Scotland let fall her black velvet gown, discovering the blood-red silk of her underbodice and petticoat. After the axe had twice fallen, the executioner shouted "God save the Queen!"—holding aloft the traitoress's head. Or so he thought; but he grasped only the auburn wig pinned to a kerchief. The wizened head, covered with grey stubble, had rolled to the edge of the platform. After twenty years of fevered machinations, the duel between Mary and Elizabeth had ended. In London bonfires blazed, bells rang, and pipes and tabors played in the streets. Shakespeare, then twenty-three and (as seems likely) newly arrived in the capital, may have watched, an interested bystander.

If Londoners greeted the tidings with rejoicing and believed, as an eyewitness sensed, that "a new era had begun in which all men would live in peace," they deluded themselves. For ironically, by eliminating her rival, Elizabeth hastened war: the next year the Armada struck. Although acceptable to Spain as a Catholic, Mary had been disadvantageously allied to the French, and the Guises (on whom she had leaned) were the dynastic rivals to the Hapsburgs. Spain's Philip II was a Hapsburg, whose Empire was roughly the sixteenth-century political equivalent of a modern industrial conglomerate. Better, he thought, to have the anti-Christ Elizabeth, excommunicated by the Pope, than Mary, the Frenchified Catholic. But now that Mary was gone, Elizabeth remained to be reckoned with. In the early days Philip had

got on tolerably well with her. He was after all Elizabeth's cousin, her sister's bereaved husband, and the erstwhile King of England (if in title only). He had entertained hopes of Elizabeth's hand. He had even been willing to put up with the stings of her free-booting privateers, of whom Sir Francis Drake—*El Draque,* the dragon, as he was called—was the most pestiferous. But he was no longer a jolly thriving wooer. Now Philip was in his sixties, hobbled by overwork, inefficient government machinery, gout, and a cataract of the eye. But his conquistadors had laden Spain's galleys with gold from the New World. Philip's religious zeal was evident both at home—where he was not remiss in burning Protestant heretics—and in America, where his missionaries offered enslaved savages the consolations of Christian salvation.

It was therefore natural enough that Philip's ponderous autocracy should spearhead the armies of the Counter-Reformation. In the Netherlands, the economic jewel of the Spanish empire, his enemies in the Reformed Church rallied around William the Silent, Prince of Orange. Philip placed a price on his head, and in 1584 an assassin's bullet at Delft silenced William forever. France, on the edge of civil war, held aloof, leaving England to sign a treaty with the United Netherlands, a pact that gave official sanction to the cause of the rebel provinces. An expeditionary force led by Leicester followed; Elizabeth had passed the point of no return.

In 1587 the Spanish ambassador in Rome laid before the gratified pontiff, Sixtus V, the grand design for an Armada that would sail that summer for England. Equipment for the Great Enterprise—including 2,431 long-muzzled culverins and 123,790 cannonballs—poured into Lisbon from the far-flung corners of the Empire. But in April *El Draque,* with a derisively small squadron, sailed unimpeded into the port of Calais, where Philip's galleons and supply craft were being refitted, and destroyed thousands of tons of shipping and stores. As he put it, Drake had singed the King of Spain's beard. Beside himself, the singed King perforce deferred the campaign until the following year. Pope Sixtus was bemused. "Just look at Drake," he exclaimed. "Who is he? What forces has he?... We are sorry to say it, but we have a poor opinion of [Philip's] Spanish Armada, and fear some disaster." Disaster was not slow in coming. Philip's Admiral, Don Alvaro de Bazán, marquis of Santa Cruz, the seasoned veteran of Spain's victory over the Turks at Lepanto, died on the eve of the expedition. In his place the King appointed Alonso Pérez de Guzmán el Bueno, Duke of Medina Sidonia and Captain General of Andalusia. An elegant aristocrat, somewhat melancholy by disposition, he was prone to colds and sea-sickness. On an Armada a person can easily catch cold, so Medina Sidonia begged to be relieved. But Philip insisted.

*Map of the English Channel showing
the Spanish Armada's approach from
the Lizard of Cornwall to the port of
Plymouth, where Sir Francis Drake first
attacked. From an atlas of European
coastal maps, THE MARINERS MIR-
ROUR (London, 1588), translated from
the Dutch of Lucas Jansz Waghenaer.*

In May 1588 the Armada set sail from Lisbon. It must have been an awesome sight: some 130 vessels. These included 20 galleons with hulls five feet thick and as many as 52 guns; 4 Italian galleases (hybrids: half galleon, half galley) of 50 guns; a second line consisting of 40 merchant-men and carracks, 34 light pinnaces; 23 *urcas* (supply ships) carrying men, horses, and siege guns; and (as last-minute reinforcements) 4 Portuguese galleys. Manning this fleet were 20,000 soldiers and 8,000 sailors, plus 1,000 gentlemen (the young Lope de Vega among them) from the proudest houses of Spain. Slaves rowed the galleys. Lacking a proper maritime service, Spain had prepared for a land battle at sea, with soldiers (rather than seamen) primed to grapple with the enemy on boarding.

Lord Howard of Effingham commanded the English fleet, with Drake as his vice-admiral and commands for Hawkins and Frobisher. This was the cream of the English navy. So far as their main fighting strength was concerned, the two sides were numerically evenly matched, each having some fifteen or sixteen men-of-war. But the English men-of-war were sleeker and lighter than their Spanish counterparts, shorn of high superstructures and ponderous castles fore and aft, but equipped with a double tier of lethal guns. The rival fleets symbolized the rival nation-states: Spain, not yet emerged from its feudal past, versus England, experimental and innovative in the flush of the Renaissance. When, half a century after Shakespeare's death, Thomas Fuller described the wit combats between nimble Shakespeare and ponderous Ben Jonson, he must have thought of the fateful naval encounter of '88 as he reached for a simile. These two, Shakespeare and Jonson, he beheld in his mind's eye as "a Spanish great galleon and an English man-of-war. Master Jonson (like the former) was built far higher in learning—solid, but slow, in his performances. Shakespeare, with the English man-of-war, lesser in bulk but lighter in sailing, could turn with all tides, tack about and take advantage of all winds." So the English did.

While the Armada sailed, Spain prayed. Each day Philip knelt for two or three hours before the Sacrament; his people gave themselves over to "processions, austerities, fasting and devotion." But God moves in mysterious ways. Storms and heavy waters scattered most of the fleet, which regrouped for repairs and revictualing at Corunna. Then, while English ships lay wind-bound at Plymouth, Captain Thomas Fleming made the first sighting of the Armada off the Lizard. That was on July 19, when Drake was playing his famous game of bowls on Plymouth Hoe. According to legend, Drake replied to the news, "We have time enough to finish the game and beat the Spaniards too." While the Spanish inexplicably delayed, the English by expert seamanship managed to get their ships out

Right: *A TRUE DISCOURSE OF THE ARMIE (London, 1588). An anonymous news account of the Spanish Armada, listing the ships, commanders, and numbers of soldiers sent against England.*

Opposite page: *SIR FRANCIS DRAKE. An engraving by Robert Boissard (ca. 1590), shown here in the first state, of which no other copy is known to exist.*

of harbor and lead them to leeward of the Eddystone. For a week the Armada in its crescent formation proceeded majestically up channel from one headland to the next. The English harassed the fleet on the flanks and to the rear, but both sides avoided a general engagement. The Spanish master plan was to team up with the forces of the Duke of Parma, the Spanish Governor of the Low Countries, who had his troops and barges waiting at Dunkirk. The united armies would then invade England under cover of the Armada. The point of rendezvous was Calais, thirty miles distant from Dunkirk.

On July 27 the Armada safely cast anchor, and news of the impending Spanish victory raced through Europe. But Parma was bottled up in the shallow harbor, and the next night Howard loosed his fireships on the Armada. The Spaniards panicked, against orders cutting their cables and putting out to sea. Their formation was broken, and vessels were scattered for miles along the Flemish coast. One of the great galleases ran aground on a sandbar. That day the decisive engagement was fought, with Drake leading almost the entire English fleet in the attack. The Spanish, heroic in combat, suffered severe losses of men, water, and supplies. After eight hours it was all over; there was nothing left but for them to head home. A sudden change in the wind allowed them to slip safely by the treacherous Dutch coast and take the outer route, via the North Sea, past the north of Scotland and west of Ireland. Many ships were wrecked against the Scottish cliffs, or sunk in the swollen surf. Thousands of men died of disease; others who straggled onto the Irish shore were massacred by the natives, possibly for their finery, possibly at the order of the Queen's lord deputy of Ireland. Around half the fleet made it back to the Tagus. The English had not lost a vessel.

Thus ended the myth of the Invincible Armada. To replace it there developed another myth which has proved more durable, that of England as an impregnable island fortress. In 1940, Adolf Hitler, a connoisseur of myths, respected it when, figuratively casting his eye across the narrow channel, he decided against invasion.

Where Shakespeare found himself during those stirring days of '88, when England waited breathless for word of the repulse, history does not record. Nor does he anywhere refer to his countrymen's triumph. Unless he is thinking of the crescent-shaped formation of the Armada when, in his 107th Sonnet, he proclaims:

> The mortal moon hath her eclipse endur'd,
> And the sad augurs mock their own presage;
> Incertainties now crown themselves assur'd,
> And peace proclaims olives of endless age.

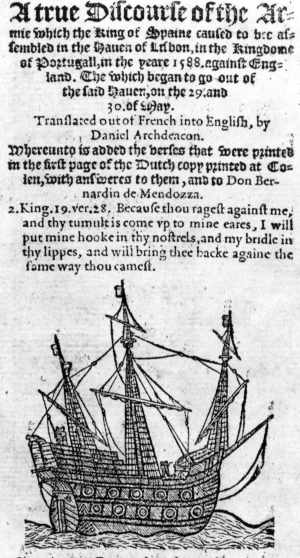

A true Discourse of the Armie which the King of Spaine caused to bee assembled in the Hauen of Lisbon, in the Kingdome of Portugall, in the yeare 1588. against England. The which began to go out of the said Hauen, on the 29. and 30. of May.

Translated out of French into English, by Daniel Archdeacon.

Whereunto is added the verses that were printed in the first page of the Dutch copy printed at Colen, with answeres to them, and to Don Bernardin de Mendozza.

2. King. 19. ver. 28. Because thou ragest against me, and thy tumult is come vp to mine eares, I will put mine hooke in thy nostrels, and my bridle in thy lippes, and will bring thee backe againe the same way thou camest.

Imprinted at London by Iohn Wolfe. 1588.

The English fleet drives the Spanish Armada from the English Channel in the decisive battle off Gravelines on Monday, July 19, 1588. An engraving by John Pine in THE TAPESTRY HANGINGS OF THE HOUSE OF LORDS: REPRESENTING THE SEVERAL ENGAGEMENTS BETWEEN THE ENGLISH AND SPANISH FLEETS IN… MDLXXXVIII (London, 1739). Commissioned by Lord Howard of Effingham (later Earl of Nottingham), England's victorious Lord High Admiral, the tapestries were hung in the House of Lords in 1616, where they remained until they were destroyed by fire in 1834.

X

DIEU ET MON DROIT

SEE

Philip prince of

Crude colored portraits of Philip II of Spain and Queen Elizabeth of England in Thomas Trevelyon's manuscript miscellany or commonplace book of 1608. Trevelyon, obviously not an artist of great talent, was probably a craftsman who compiled his book for his own edi- *fication and amusement. It contains decorative alphabets and embroidery patterns, as well as portraits of historical, Biblical, and allegorical figures. Many were undoubtedly copied from popular prints and broadsides no longer in existence.*

But whether or not Shakespeare alludes to the defeat of the Armada—and the intriguing suggestion has persuaded few—there can be no question about his reference to the last great event of Elizabeth's reign. In the Prologue to the final act of *Henry V*, the Chorus describes the response of the London populace to the return of their conquering Caesar from the field of Agincourt, likening it to the reception soon to be accorded another military hero:

> Were now the General of our gracious Empress—
> As in good time he may—from Ireland coming,
> Bringing rebellion broached on his sword,
> How many would the peaceful city quit
> To welcome him!

Henry V first saw performance in 1599. On March 27th of that year, Robert Devereux, second Earl of Essex, set forth with a puissant force on his Irish expedition. He was then at the apogee of his fame, and on the brink of disaster. For him, as for so many others, character was fate. Handsomely proportioned, this tall young aristocrat with soulful brown eyes and full, sensual lips had burst upon the Court fifteen years earlier, when he was not quite eighteen. He brought the right credentials for entrée: his grandfather, Sir Francis Knollys, was the Queen's cousin; his stepfather, the Earl of Leicester, her beloved Robin. Impulsive and petulant, generous but vindictive, arrogant, envious, given to sulking when denied his way, he had what a later age would term charisma. In the Earl of Essex, the spirit of chivalry seemed to be reborn. But so did other, less positive, attributes of the past. A feudal baron, Essex failed to appreciate that he lived in a nation state. Nor, with his traditional attitude of masculine superiority toward women, did he reckon adequately with the power of the female, grown old and decayed in the tooth, who held sway over him. But Essex's chief drawback was that he did not have a head on his shoulders. So at the last he lost it on the executioner's block.

Before the end of 1587 Essex had succeeded his stepfather (soon to die in the Armada year) as Master of the Horse. A few months later he was installed as Knight of the Garter. These preferments he did not always wear well. When the Queen rewarded Sir Charles Blount with a gold chess-queen for running well at the tilt, and that amiable young aristocrat wore it the next day at Court, Essex insulted him. "Now I perceive every fool must have a favor," he snarled. In the inevitable duel the Earl was wounded. Elizabeth did not grieve. "God's death!" she exploded, "it was fit that some one or other should take him down and teach him better manners, otherwise there will be no rule with him." Essex lived extravagantly, incurred debts, and played truant from Court by sailing off with Drake on an expedition to Por-

coupled tgether wyth halters about their neck pardened them all; the second yeare of here ra es day the marriag was solemnysed betweene spaine and queene mary, the .28. day of no was made for the queene and bruted that with child; 1554. the .21. day of march doc was burned at oxford, in the yeare .1556. ar of her raigne the .27. day of June .13. po at stratford the bowe; queene mary died november in the yeare of our lord .1558. igned .5. yeares .4. monethes and ode dayes and we

Philip prince of spayne was married to quee

...yne

queene .....
n saynt Jam-
rince .of
. prayer
as quycke
rannnor -
. 4 . yeare
were burnt
7 . day of
she had ra-
d at westmyn

y the second

Queene Elizabeth

yeare of the queenes raigne one saynt James day 1555

Elyzabeth queene of england second daughter to kyng henry
the eight to the great comfort of england, was proclamed
queene the 17 day of november, in the yeare of lord 1558 the
15 day of January the queene was crowned at westmynster by
doctor oglethorpe byshop of carlyle; in the theird yeare of the
queenes raigne ane Jmoore professed to be christ our saviour,
and the same Jmoore was whipped till hee confessed christ to be

tuguese Corunna. It failed. Nonetheless, the Queen received Essex back to favor, as she would do more than once again. Perhaps she was just a foolish old spinster infatuated with an unstable young suitor whose brilliant, moody company she evidently enjoyed. As for Essex, he made the mistake of overestimating his appeal for decayed maidens.

Essex sought glory through arms, but mainly it eluded him. In 1591, for example, he led a small expedition to aid in the siege of Rouen. The governor unsportingly passed up the Earl's invitation to personal combat, and even refused to yield the town. Easily bored, Essex left his infantry vulnerably behind him in order to go off and play leapfrog—literally—with the King of France. In this contest he proved victorious. When Essex returned to England he was disappointed to find his monarch disappointed. In 1596 he was off with Sir Walter Ralegh to strike at Cadiz. With splendid bravery he led his men in scaling the walls of the port, then with equally splendid magnanimity spared the inhabitants. Not their possessions, however; these the English looted, for themselves rather than for the Crown. When Essex re-greeted his Queen, he had only a newly sprouted beard to show for his campaign. But he was now a national hero.

He played the game of politics with equally mixed results. Essex became, in succession, Privy Councilor, Master of the Ordnance, and Earl Marshall. But in July 1598 he flared up dangerously over the appointment of a new Lord Deputy for Ireland, and in the presence of Nottingham, Cecil, and a clerk of the signet, unceremoniously turned his back on the Queen. Even more unceremoniously, she boxed his ears. His hand moved to his sheathed sword, but Nottingham intervened, and the hothead left in high dudgeon. They managed to patch things up.

Meanwhile the man Essex fancied to be his arch-rival moved methodically up the ladder of power and preferment. This was Robert Cecil, the delicate hunchbacked son of Elizabeth's most trusted councilor, then Lord Burghley. Usually the Queen advanced Cecil while Essex was away: admitting him to her Council while the Earl played leapfrog in France, appointing him Secretary during the Cadiz expedition, making him Master of the Wards (a remunerative post carrying a power base) when her erstwhile favorite was off in Ireland. Essex's athleticism and good looks proved no match for prudence; Cecil had a head on his shoulders.

Only once, and then not creditably, did the Earl triumph over his rival. It was Essex who pursued the Queen's Portuguese physician, Dr. Lopez, a converted Jew, to the scaffold, on grounds of his supposed implication in a conspiracy to poison her. Cecil thought Lopez innocent. Elizabeth was unpersuaded of his guilt, and tried to have him kept under her protection in the Tower. To no avail. On June 7, 1594, Lopez was hanged after declaring from the gallows (as an eyewitness recorded) "that he loved the Queen as well as he loved Jesus Christ, which coming from a man of the Jewish profession moved no small laughter in the standers-by."

Not very long after this event, Shakespeare wrote a play featuring a Devil Jew who is yet human. In the great trial scene in *The Merchant of Venice* Gratiano excoriates Shylock:

> Thy currish spirit
> Govern'd a wolf who, hang'd for human slaughter,
> Even from the gallows did his fell soul fleet,
> And, whilst thou layest in thy unhallowed dam,
> Infus'd itself in thee; for thy desires
> Are wolfish, bloody, starv'd, and ravenous.

It is perhaps stretching a point to find in these lines an allusion to the execution of Lopez, but "wolf" (capitalized in the early Quarto text) puns, via translation, on his name. We are told that "Lopez was popularly known as Doctor Lopus... and from Lopus to Lupus is no great step."

Be that as it may, when *Henry V* with its patriotic theme first made pulses quicken at the newly inaugurated Globe playhouse, the Irish, rather than the Jewish, question was agitating Englishmen. That "base bush kern"—as Elizabeth derisively termed Hugh O'Neill, Earl of Tyrone—had humiliated the occupying army, and was threatening Dublin itself. Essex engineered his own appointment as general of an expeditionary force to attack Tyrone in Ulster, hoping to return a revalidated hero. To this end he sallied forth with sixteen thousand foot soldiers and thirteen hundred cavalry, the largest English force yet dispatched to Ireland. "By God, I will beat Tyrone in the field," Essex vaunted to Sir John Harington; "for nothing worthy her Majesty's honor hath yet been achieved." But second thoughts assailed him. "Into Ireland I go," he sighed. "The Queen hath irrevocably decreed it, the Council do passionately urge it, and I am tied by my own reputation to use no tergiversation." If Ireland loomed as a crucible to prove a brave man's mettle, it was also, he realized, a Hibernian bog into which many a brave man had sunk.

The Right Honorable Robert Devorex
Earle of Essex and ewe Earle Marshall
of England, her Mᵃ. Lieutenant and go-
uerner generall of the Kingdom of Ireland
Vicount hereford and bourgcher, Lord
seres of Chartley bourgcher and louan
Mayster of her Mᵃ. Horse and of her
Ordinance, Knight of the most noble order
of the garter, and of her highnes prinie
Counsell, and Chauncellor of the
Vniuersitie of Cambridge.

IRELANDE

The Ilands
of Treceràs.
Coruo, Sᵗ George. Trecera
Flores,
Faiall. Pico

The English Fleet,

ROAN

CADIZ

A. 1596.

BASIS
VIRTVTVM
CONSTANTIÆ

HONI SOIT QVI MAL Y PENSE

Vertues honor, Wisdomes ualure, Graces seruaunt, Mercies loue,
Gods elected, Truths beloued, Heauens affected. Doe all a proue. Tocksonus.
fecit.

So it would prove for Essex. He frittered away precious time and huge sums of money—the expedition cost Elizabeth £300,000—while attrition sapped his forces to a fraction of their strength. Wracked by pain from the stone and harboring treasonous thoughts, Essex made a sham march against Tyrone. Then on September 7, 1599, he held a secret parley with the base kern at a ford. While Tyrone sat bareheaded in midstream on his horse, Essex from the opposite bank negotiated an ignominious truce. Renouncing the Ulster campaign, the Earl then spurred posthaste back to the Court at Nonsuch, bursting in, mud-besplattered, on the Queen in her bedchamber as she was dressing, her hair about her ears. Her Majesty was not amused.

If the Irish campaign ended as farce, what followed was tragedy. The Queen moved circumspectly. Essex was still a popular hero, with a following among the young blades he had (as his military office allowed) promiscuously made knights. Instead of confining him to prison, therefore, and thus conferring martyrdom, she placed him in the hands of a friendly councilor, Lord Keeper Egerton. When Essex fell ill, she sent him hot soup. On Cecil's advice (why he so advised remains a mystery), she canceled the public trial designed for her vindication. But, as slanderous rumors persisted, alleging that Essex had been condemned unheard, she had him hailed before a special commission that stripped him of his offices and sentenced him to detention. When his lease of the customs on sweet wines—the financial prop of his estate—expired, she declined to renew it. But rather than award this perquisite to another, she awaited evidence of Essex's reformation. She waited in vain.

After regaining his freedom in August 1600, Essex brought together a motley crew of malcontents, fortune-hunters, and swaggerers at Essex House. In early February they marched to seize the Court, the Tower, and the City. The Queen, they reckoned—fantasized, rather—would bow to their will. But the populace failed to rise in Essex's behalf, and he was left with no choice except to barricade himself in his mansion overlooking the Thames. Surrender, trial, and execution quickly followed. Essex was thirty-four when he met death with dignity, all passion spent, in the courtyard of the Tower.

Shakespeare's company and one of Shakespeare's plays played their parts in the February drama. For a bonus of forty shillings paid by Sir Gelly Meyrick, one of the conspirators, the troupe revived an old favorite, *Richard II,* at the Globe the day before the insurrection. A company of the Earl's followers crossed the Thames to take heart from watching a depiction of the successful deposition of an anointed prince. The Queen did not punish the Lord Chamberlain's Men for its indiscretion; indeed, the troupe played before her on the eve of Essex's execution. She was, in general, clement. Only five of the ringleaders met death; others were fined. But time failed to assuage the aged Queen's bitterness. In August, as she sat in her Privy Chamber in East Greenwich, she remarked to the Keeper of the Records of the Tower, "I am Richard II, know ye not that?" To which he diplomatically replied, "Such a wicked imagination was determined and attempted by a most unkind gentleman, the most adorned creature that ever your Majesty made." She had, as usual, the last word: "He that will forget God, will also forget his benefactors; this tragedy was played forty times in open streets and houses." Thus did Elizabeth take note of the seditious potency of art.

The woman who reminisced in this fashion was then nearing seventy. Elizabeth had reigned for almost half a century; most of her subjects had known no other ruler. There was nothing in her life that could any longer give her pleasure, she confided to the French ambassador. Yet despite the seated melancholy accompanying her advanced years, she was blessed with exceptional health: one fine day in 1602 she rode ten miles on horseback, and hunted as well. She enjoyed music and dancing and the players. But toward the end a heavy dullness and lethargy overtook the Queen. "I am not sick," she mused, "I feel no pain, and yet I pine away." She ordered her coronation ring, signifying her marriage to England, filed from her finger—so deeply imbedded had it become in her flesh. Another ring which Essex, while her reigning favorite, had given her, she still wore. Finally, on March 24, 1603, she died, "easily," in the words of one memorialist, falling away "like a ripe apple from a tree." Only (report holds) at the very end, as she sat dying—she refused to take to a bed from which she would never rise—did she name a successor: her cousin James VI of Scotland, whose mother Mary she had in times past dueled to the death.

At thirty-six and in his prime, James was the logical choice: male, Protestant, yet (by virtue of his mother's allegiance) acceptable to Catholic interests. He had an indisputable dynastic claim, and sons to maintain it. As a Scot he was intriguingly foreign, yet not outlandishly exotic. Essex had sought to seduce James with a crack-brained project by which he would raise an army and, marching to the Borders, assert his right to the throne. But prudently James had resisted temptation. When the great moment at last arrived, the indispensable Cecil drafted the proclamation making him James I of England. Bonfires, the inevitable accompaniment to such occasions, blazed in the streets of London. Sir Robert Carey posted to Holyrood with the tidings that ushered in a new age of kings.

On April 5, savoring his position as the wayfarer who had for years wandered "in a wilderness and barren soil" and had "now arrived at the land of promise," James ventured forth on the long journey south to claim his inheritance. He had never crossed the border before. Along the way the curious gaped at his unprepossessing figure. Of middle height, with broad shoulders and a thin, square beard, James had sandy hair, a nose too big for his face and a tongue too big for his puckered mouth. His skin bore a girlish softness, and his legs were so bent and spindly from a childhood bout with rickets that he required assistance when he walked. Not surprisingly, he preferred to ride. If James seemed corpulent, that was because he wore a thickly padded doublet to safeguard his royal body from would-be assassins' daggers. The new King reluctantly placed himself on view. In this respect, as in others, he differed from his predecessor. He "did not caress the people nor make them that good cheer the late Queen did, whereby she won their loves," observed the Venetian ambassador. James himself made the point less diplomatically. "God's wounds!" he expostulated when notified that his subjects wished to see him, "I will pull down my breeches and they shall also see my arse." Had he done so, they would have glimpsed perhaps his best feature.

Expectant hordes thronged the capital for the coronation scheduled to take place that summer. "The streets," we hear, "were plumed with gallants, tobacconists filled up whole taverns, vintners hung out spick-and-span new ivy bushes." But once again pestilence gripped London, even more severely this time than in the previous decade. Each week more than eleven hundred were dying in the city and suburbs. Inevitably, the authorities barred the general public from the ceremonies at which, on July 25th, the first Stuart was crowned at Westminster. The royal progress through the streets, for which the municipal fathers had made elaborate preparations, was canceled; workmen took down the seven Arches of Triumph laboriously erected at great cost. The arches rose again the next year, however, after the plague had abated.

On March 15, 1604, between eleven and noon, the royal entourage—the King, his consort Anne, and their son Prince Henry—left the Tower and proceeded with solemn pomp along streets lined by guildsmen in their colorful liveries. At each of the arches, which were fantastically bedecked with carvings, the mightiest of princes and royalest of kings was greeted with orations by allegorical personages representing Genius Urbis, Peace, Zeal, and the like. Music played, choruses sang, conduits ran claret wine. The speeches proved mostly inaudible; some (as the day wore on) were omitted. Typical was the ceremony that took place at the Cross in Cheap. The arch here represented *Hortus Euporiae,* the Garden of Plenty. Garnished with fruit and flowers, it offered Fortune at the top, Peace and Plenty seated below, and—stretched across either end—the Seven Liberal Arts and the Muses holding musical instruments. A voice sang in praise of the King's regenerative powers:

> O this is he!
> Whose new beams make our spring,
> Men glad and birds to sing,
> Hymns of praise, joy, and glee.

To which the massed chorus "in full voice" added the refrain, "Sing, sing, O this is he!" Through it all James listened glumly, without essaying any impromptu speeches of response. "He endured the day's brunt with patience," an observer noted, "being assured he should never have another."

But if bourgeois street theatre, representing the lower end of the theatrical spectrum, was not to the royal taste, the plays acted by the professional companies were something else. Within ten days of his arrival in the capital, the new King had instructed Cecil, as Keeper of the Privy Seal, to prepare letters patent under the Great Seal of England for Shakespeare's troupe. Thus, by a royal patent enrolled on May 19, 1603, did the Lord Chamberlain's Men become the King's Men—a designation tacitly acknowledging their preeminence. The actors were now literally His Majesty's servants. As a Groom of the Chamber, each member of the company received, in anticipation of the 1604 progress through London, an allotment of scarlet-red cloth for his livery. Shakespeare and his companions, however, seem not to have marched in the procession alongside the nobles and courtiers and state functionaries present that March day, for accounts of the Magnificent Entertainment, some written by theatre folk, fail to mention their presence.

The King's Men acted at Court the following Christmas, when they performed several of Shakespeare's pieces, including the lately composed *Measure for Measure*. This play, in which an untested magistrate is obliged to cope with age-old questions of justice and mercy, had an obvious topical relevance, there being a new and untested ruler, interested in such problems, on the throne. Some have seen in the play's Duke of Vienna a flattering portrait of James. Vincentio, like James, abhors crowds. "I'll privily away," he confides to Angelo.

> I love the people,
> But do not like to stage me to their eyes;
> Though it do well, I do not relish well
> Their loud applause and Aves vehement;
> Nor do I think the man of safe discretion
> That does affect it.

Such sentiments James would have recognized and applauded. Presumably, too, James would have been pleased to see how closely the views on statecraft depicted in *Measure for Measure* resemble those propounded by James himself in his *Basilicon Doron,* or "kingly gift." Some learned commentators have gone so far as to suggest that Shakespeare himself acted the Duke before His Majesty at Whitehall. Little wonder that we have been invited to accept, as one critic wittily puts it, a King James version of *Measure for Measure.*

So too *Macbeth,* which followed a couple of years later, reflects its Jacobean genesis. Shakespeare had turned before to Raphael Holinshed's *Chronicle of England, Scotland, and Ireland,* drawing on its narratives for his grandly sweeping dramatization of English history from the deposition of Richard II to the triumph of Henry Tudor on Bosworth Field. But never before—or after—did a Scottish theme fire his imagination. His sovereign traced his own descent from Banquo; James is therefore appropriately represented in the prophetic Show of Eight Kings conjured up by the witches. The cooperation between England and Scotland demonstrated in *Macbeth* would presumably appeal to a monarch who dreamed of uniting the two kingdoms. And as for the Weird Sisters themselves, had not James written learnedly on the nature and perils of witchcraft in his *Demonology?* From these considerations it is but an easy leap to seeing *Macbeth* as a royal play. Speculation holds that Shakespeare composed it especially for the visit to England of Queen Anne's brother, Christian IV of Denmark, in July 1606.

The date suits, but this occasion, in keeping with the already established reputation of James's court for sottishness as well as Scottishness, was notable more for hard-drinking than exalted playgoing. "Our feasts were magnificent, and the two royal guests did most lovingly embrace each other at table," observed Sir John Harington, an eyewitness. "I think the Dane hath strangely wrought on our good English nobles; for those, whom I never could get to taste good liquor, now follow the fashion and wallow in beastly delights. The ladies abandon their sobriety, and are seen to roll about in intoxication." At one entertainment the lady playing the Queen of Sheba spilled her rich present of wine, cream, and jelly into the Danish King's royal lap; undismayed, he lurched up to dance with her, only to fall and be carried off to bed in an inner chamber. In the same allegorical show Charity mumbled some of her lines, then staggered out to join Faith and Hope, who were spewing in the lower hall. Harington's wonderful sanitary invention, had it then been available, would no doubt have been much appreciated. The festivities give an unforeseen point to Hamlet the Dane's advice to his friend, "We'll teach you to drink deep ere you depart."

Macbeth at such revels? In the absence of any performance record, that hardly seems likely. Nor is there persuasive evidence that any of Shakespeare's plays—including *Measure for Measure*—was written with a particular courtly occasion in mind. However tempting it is to envisage Shakespeare as hobnobbing with the movers and shakers in the corridors of power, courtly rewards were merely bonuses. His, and his company's, bread and butter came from the anonymous masses who paid their pennies to applaud universal themes, incomparably expressed, in a cavernous open-air amphitheatre on Bankside.

Yet a poet of Shakespeare's unique sensibility and inquiring intellect could not have remained indifferent to the quality of life under the first Stuart. And that quality left something to be desired. James had a passion for the chase, to which, with his horses and hounds, he devoted many hours. Also for his favorites, who were inevitably male. That he was in fact homosexual has never been proven, but his indecorums with his minions raised eyebrows. "Nor was his love," as Francis Osborne caustically summed up, "or what else posterity will please to call it (who must be the judges of all that history shall inform) carried on with a discretion sufficient to cover a less scandalous behavior; for the King's kissing them after so lascivious a mode in public, and upon the throne, as it were, of the world, prompted many to imagine some things done in the tiring house that exceed my expression, no less than they do my experience." The more refined courtly diversions, such as dancing and music, James disliked. His manners were coarse, his dress slovenly. "He never washed his hands," wrote Sir Anthony Welden, "only rubbed his fingers' ends slightly with the wet end of a napkin." When he rose from table, his ungainly bearing became even more evident. "His walk was ever circular," wrote a contemporary, "his fingers

ELIZABETH, QUEEN OF BOHEMIA, by the Dutch painter Michiel Janszoon van Mierevelt. Elizabeth was the eldest daughter of James I, and her wedding in 1613 to Frederick, Elector Palatine, was the occasion of many festivities at Court, including the performance of several of Shakespeare's plays, JULIUS CAESAR and THE TEMPEST among them. The portrait probably dates from about the time of her marriage.

ever in that walk fiddling about his codpiece."

As kings go, he had been poor. But that was in the barren north. The English coffers would prove inexhaustible, he reckoned—mistakenly, as he discovered after prodigally emptying them. Not that he waged costly wars. Military types frightened him; when a soldier once offered to kiss his hand, the story goes, the King snatched it away, saying he feared it might be bitten. *"Beati pacifici"* was his motto. For keeping England at peace throughout the twenty-two years of his reign, James was widely regarded as a coward.

He preferred to see himself as the British Solomon. At the age of eight he had impressed the English ambassador by his ability to translate random passages from the Latin Bible extemporaneously into French and English. Verse he valued and dabbled in, publishing at eighteen his *Essays of a Prentice in the Divine Art of Poesy.* He translated Ariosto, fancied himself a theologian, and wrote voluminously on a variety of subjects: religious polemics, the evils of tobacco, the divine right of kings. Witches fascinated James; dueling alarmed him. So his outpourings testify. But if James fancied himself a savant, he was in truth a pedant. Yet his bookishness won the admiration of the great French humanist Isaac Casaubon. "He is a lover of learning to a degree beyond belief," Casaubon recorded; "his judgment of books, old and new, is such as would become a professional scholar, rather than a mighty prince." Others felt differently, including Henry IV of France, who, persuaded that the making of books was no fit occupation for a king, allowed that James was the wisest fool in Christendom.

"O Hamlet, what a falling off was there," exclaims Shakespeare's Ghost, one monarch comparing himself with another. Historians have gravely shaken their heads over the glory that departed, never to return, when the crown passed from Elizabeth to James. They have a point. Still, one could make a case for the first decade of the Jacobean age as the incandescent moment of the English Renaissance. That decade saw the first flowering of the metaphysical mode in the wittily impassioned songs and sonnets of John Donne. Incarcerated in the Tower as a troublesome anachronism, Sir Walter Ralegh labored away at his magisterially eloquent *History of the World,* published in a sumptuous folio in 1614. The King's Men acted Ben Jonson's masterpieces, *Volpone* and *The Alchemist.* Beginning with *The Masque of Blackness* presented on Twelfth Night in 1605, Jonson collaborated with Inigo Jones, architect and stage-designer extraordinary, on a series of masques that brought this species of court entertainment to its apogee. Shakespeare continued regularly turning out new plays each year, some of them among his greatest: *King Lear, Antony and Cleopatra, The Tempest.*

The royal state visit of Marie de Medici, Queen Mother of France. An engraving in Jean Puget de la Serre's HISTOIRE DE L'ENTRÉE DE LA REYNE MERE DU ROY TRÈS-CHRESTIEN DANS LA GRANDE BRETAIGNE (London, 1639). This procession past Cheapside offers a good background view of London's closely-crowded half-timbered houses before the great fire of 1666.

TRES-CHRESTIEN DANS LA VILLE DE LO

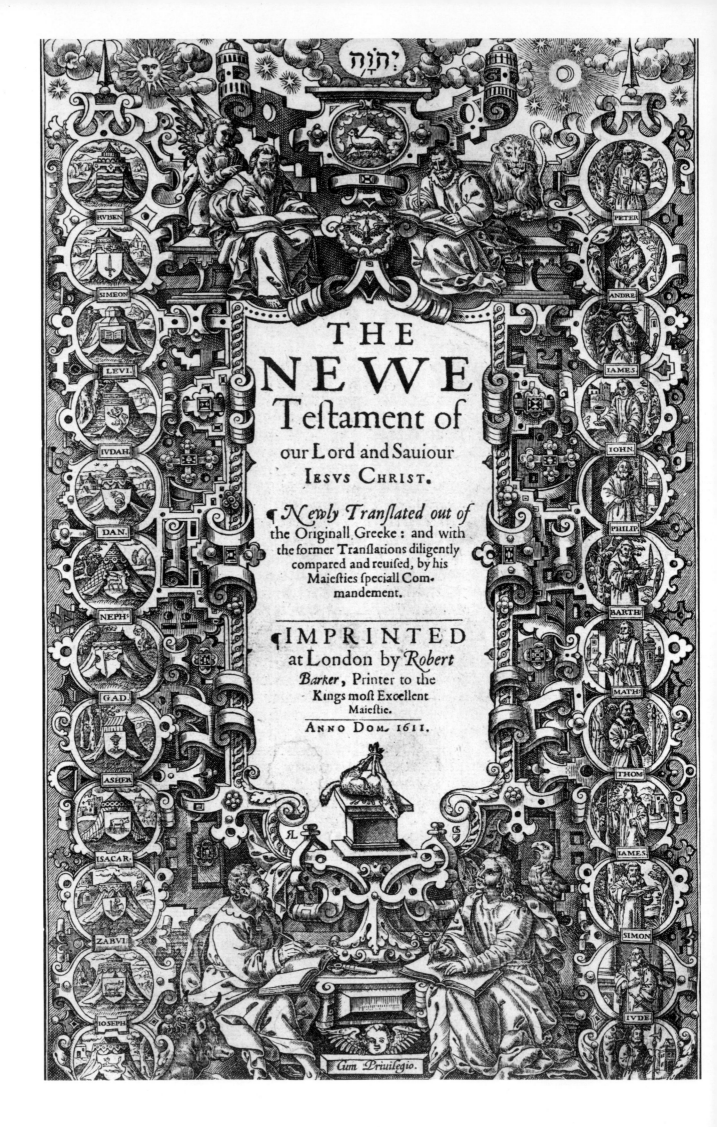

יהוה

THE
NEWE
Testament of
our Lord and Sauiour
IESVS CHRIST.

¶ Newly Translated out of
the Originall Greeke: and with
the former Translations diligently
compared and reuised, by his
Maiesties speciall Com-
mandement.

¶IMPRINTED
at London by Robert
Barker, Printer to the
Kings most Excellent
Maiestie.
ANNO DOM. 1611.

Cum Priuilegio.

Opposite page: *Title page of the New Testament in the first edition of the KING JAMES BIBLE (London, 1611). A revision of the Bible begun in 1604 by a group of 54 clergymen with the encouragement of the monarch, the King James version was never officially authorized. Owing to its own merit, however, it became the most generally used version of the Bible and a monument of the English language. This is the issue known as the "He Bible" for the reading in Ruth iii. 15, "he went into the city." The later, accepted, version reads "she went."*

This page: *Engraved portrait of Sir Walter Ralegh from the title page of his HISTORY OF THE WORLD (London, 1617). The HISTORY was written while Ralegh was confined in the Tower of London on a charge of treason against James I. Courtier, soldier, sailor, and explorer, Ralegh is chiefly remembered in America for his attempt to found the first English colony in Virginia.*

Dissatisfied with the antimonarchical bias of the marginal notes ("very partial, untrue, seditious, and savoring too much of dangerous conceits") of the Genevan Bible then in most general use, James set forth a program for a new translation to be undertaken by the most accomplished linguists of the universities of Oxford and Cambridge, reviewed after completion by the bishops and other learned prelates, then submitted to the Privy Council, and finally ratified by royal prerogative. From this program emerged, in 1611, the King James Version of the Bible. Together, Shakespeare and the King James Version transformed for all succeeding generations the topography of the English language.

Those drawn to odious comparisons of Elizabethan and Jacobean must acknowledge that some giants survived the Scottish flood. The survivors fared diversely. Physically puny as giants go, Cecil proved the most resilient, making himself for his politic wisdom no less necessary to the new sovereign than he had been to the old. Cecil stayed on as Secretary of State, became Lord Treasurer, and was apotheosized as Earl of Salisbury. Francis Bacon dedicated his *Advancement of Learning* to a King greedy of learning, but failed to persuade him of the importance of the Baconian inductive method for exploring the labyrinth of nature. Bacon's worldly career flourished nevertheless. As Attorney General, he carried weight; James made him Lord Chancellor, and created him Viscount St. Albans. In the end his enemies brought him down on charges of bribery and corruption, to which he freely confessed. Bacon's career thus exemplifies the perils he had so brilliantly described in his early essay "Of Great Place":

> The rising unto place is laborious; and by pains men come to greater pains; and it is sometimes base; and by indignities, men come to dignities. The standing is slippery, and the regress is either a downfall, or at least an eclipse, which is a melancholy thing.

But under James no star suffered a more melancholy eclipse than Sir Walter Ralegh's.

No star had burned more brightly. Soldier, sailor, and courtier, Ralegh probed both the New World opened up by the voyagers and the interior continent of his own psyche. He financed and masterminded the first colonization of Virginia. As a poet, he penned an urbanely cynical reply to Marlowe's celebrated lyric, "Come live with me and be my love," and hymned the ocean's praise of Cynthia, his chaste moon-goddess Queen. A generous patron of poets, he received the author's letter prefacing the first three books of the age's most notable non-dramatic poem, *The Faerie Queene*. But Ralegh was also proud, overbearing, and of a cruel heart, the last exemplified by his massacre in cold blood of the garrison at

San José. He was larger than life—a Renaissance man whose career would have made a fitting subject for a Shakespearean tragedy.

In the eighties—his glory days—Ralegh was Elizabeth's reigning favorite. He had risen from provincial obscurity to be, he boasted in a letter, "believed not inferior to any man, to pleasure or displeasure the greatest"; and, he went on, "my opinion is so received and believed as I can anger the best of them." Ralegh incurred disgrace by seducing one of the Queen's maids of honor, Elizabeth Throckmorton, whom he secretly married while imprisoned in the Tower. He regained favor, however, when his English fleet captured the Portuguese carrack, *Madre de Dios,* which yielded the richest booty ever taken in such an exploit. In 1595 Ralegh set out on a dangerous voyage of exploration along the coast of South America in pursuit of the legendary New Hesperides, the Golden Apples of the sun—or, as some called it, El Dorado. On his return the next year, he published *The Discovery of the Large, Rich and Beautiful Empire of Guiana, with a relation of the Great and Golden City of Manoa (which the Spaniards call El Dorado) and of the provinces of Emeria, Arromaia, Amapaia, and other Countries, with their Rivers Adjoining.*

In his wonderfully cadenced prose Ralegh described the wonders he had seen: "the grass short and green, and in divers parts groves of trees by themselves, as if they had been by all the art and labor in the world so made of purpose: and still as we rowed, the deer came down feeding by the water's side, as if they had been used to a keeper's call." But the expedition brought back only a handful of gold or gold-bearing ore—the name of the game—and his report was received *cum grano.* With his arrogant bearing and reputation for free-thinking, this swarthy swaggerer in his extravagant cloaks and ruffs had become the most hated man at Court. He might have said, with Shakespeare's Richard III, "I am myself alone."

The new dispensation brought his downfall. As regards Spain, Ralegh belonged to the war party, whereas James was a prince of peace. The King had sat on the throne only a few months when, at a scandalously unfair trial, Ralegh was convicted of high treason and sentenced to execution. But the verdict was not carried out, and for years the supreme activist lived in comfortable captivity in the Tower, pursuing his scientific and philosophical inquiries. Once he was even called upon to prescribe a remedy when Prince Charles fell ill. Finally in 1617, at the advanced age (for those days) of sixty-five, Ralegh secured his conditional release by promising the financially hard-pressed King a gold mine in Guiana, to be obtained without trespassing on the Spanish colony there. The mission was foredoomed to failure. Ralegh's son met death in a skirmish with the Spanish settlers, his chief officer committed suicide, the men mutinied.

When the survivors found their way back to England, the old sentence of execution hanging over Ralegh was reinstated at the pleasure of the Spanish ambassador. "All is vanity and weariness," Ralegh acknowledged near the end—but "such a weariness and vanity that we shall ever complain of it and love it for all that." On his last morning Sir Walter Ralegh smoked his last pipe of the tobacco he had introduced into England. On the scaffold, he admonished his trembling headsman, "What dost thou fear? Strike, man, strike!" In the New World, Ralegh's name lives on as the capital city of North Carolina, one of the colonies his enterprise helped to found.

Ralegh was but one of many fabulous voyagers who sailed previously uncharted seas. Most had earlier passed from the scene. On January 28, 1595, Sir Francis Drake had died of yellow fever aboard his flagship off Nombre de Dios in Panama. *The Golden Hind,* the fragile bark on which with his happy few he had circumnavigated the globe in an epic three-year journey, lay moldering at Deptford, where the Queen had knighted him on board ship after his triumphant return. Thomas Cavendish had repeated the exploit in his "admirable and prosperous voyage" of the Armada year, but he too succumbed to yellow fever, at the age of thirty-one or thirty-two, in the general disaster that overtook his second voyage, the object of which was to open direct trade between England and China. These and other daring spirits—among others, Gilbert, who had claimed Newfoundland for the Queen, Frobisher, who had sailed to the Arctic—made the Elizabethan age the Age of Exploration. By the time of James's accession the enterprise seemed to have sputtered

Opposite page: *English readers were introduced to the tobacco plant through this woodcut in Nicholas Monardes's JOYFULL NEWES OUT OF THE NEWE FOUNDE WORLDE (London, 1577), translated from the Spanish by John Frampton.*

Below: *Royal warrant of James I for the release of Sir Walter Ralegh from the Tower of London, January 30, 1617. The great seal of the King is attached to the vellum document. Upon his release, Ralegh set forth on his final disastrous voyage to the New World.*

out. No English settlers remained alive in North America. John White's colony at Roanoke Island had mysteriously disappeared. "We let fall our grapnel near the shore," records Governor White, who landed with a relief expedition in August 1590, "and sounded with a trumpet call, and afterwards many familiar English tunes of songs, and called to them friendly; but we had no answer." All they found were some old cannonballs and buried chests, and the remains of fort and houses.

Under James the seed was replanted and bore new fruit. A second generation of heroes contributed to the drama of exploration. In 1608 Captain John Smith and his party, sailing three thousand miles in an open boat, investigated both sides of the Chesapeake Bay and went up the Potomac River to where Washington now stands. Smith is best known, of course, for his escape from imminent execution by the Indians who had captured him, when Princess Pocahontas, then a child of twelve or thirteen, pleaded with her father, the great chief Powhatan, to spare him. The story is probably more than pure romance. "At the minute of my execution," Smith addressed Queen Anne in 1616, "she hazarded the beating out of her own brains to save mine."

The first of her tribe to convert to Christianity, Pocahontas was received as a celebrity at the English court that year. John Chamberlain, newsmonger, records the visit: "The Virginian woman Pocahontas with her father councellor have been with the King and graciously used, and both she and her assistant well placed at the masque; she is upon her return (though sore against her will) if the wind will come about to send her away." The gorgeous masque she attended was Ben Jonson's *Vision of Delight,* performed on January 6 and 19, 1617. Years later, Jonson referred to her in *The Staple of News*

(1626), when his Penniboy Canter mentions having seen a princess at a tavern:

> The blessed
> Pocahontas (as the historian calls her)
> And great king's daughter of Virginia
> Hath been in womb of a tavern.

The thought of Pocahontas raising a pint in a London pub is intriguing. In the event, the fair wind for her return to Virginia never came. At Gravesend in March, she died, a casualty—neither the first nor the last—of the English climate. She was twenty-two.

Her visit took place after Shakespeare's death. Late in his career, he had in *The Tempest* responded imaginatively to the new vistas opened up by exploration. Paradoxically he confined himself (as he had not done since his youthful *Comedy of Errors*) to the neoclassic unities of time and place and set his exotic scene, at least technically, in the Old World. The Italian mariners suffer their shipwreck on a homeward journey to Naples from the marriage of Claribel, the King's daughter, in Tunis. Thus geography points to the Mediterranean. But no European sun ever set on these yellow sands:

> The isle is full of noises,
> Sounds, and sweet airs, that give delight, and hurt not.
> Sometimes a thousand twangling instruments
> Will hum about mine ears; and sometimes voices,
> That, if I then had wak'd after long sleep,
> Will make me sleep again; and then, in dreaming,
> The clouds methought would open and show riches
> Ready to drop upon me, that, when I wak'd,
> I cried to dream again.

Below: *The adventures of Captain John Smith in Virginia, during the years 1606 to 1609, a plate in his* GENERALL HISTORIE OF VIRGINIA *(London, 1624). The engraving at the lower right shows Pocahontas saving Smith's life.*

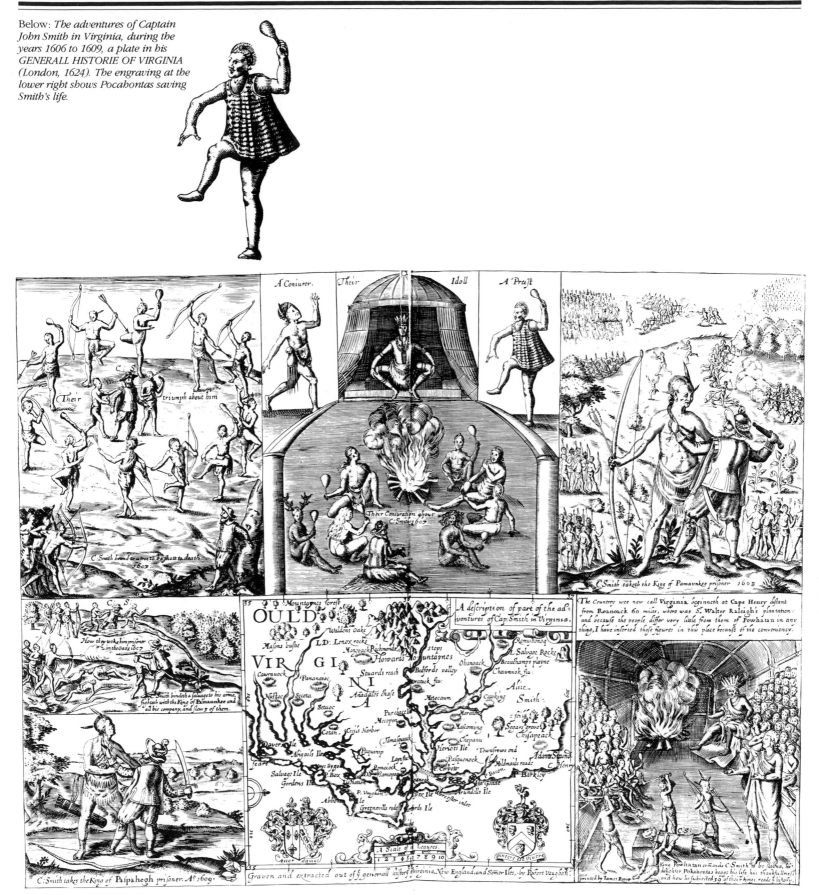

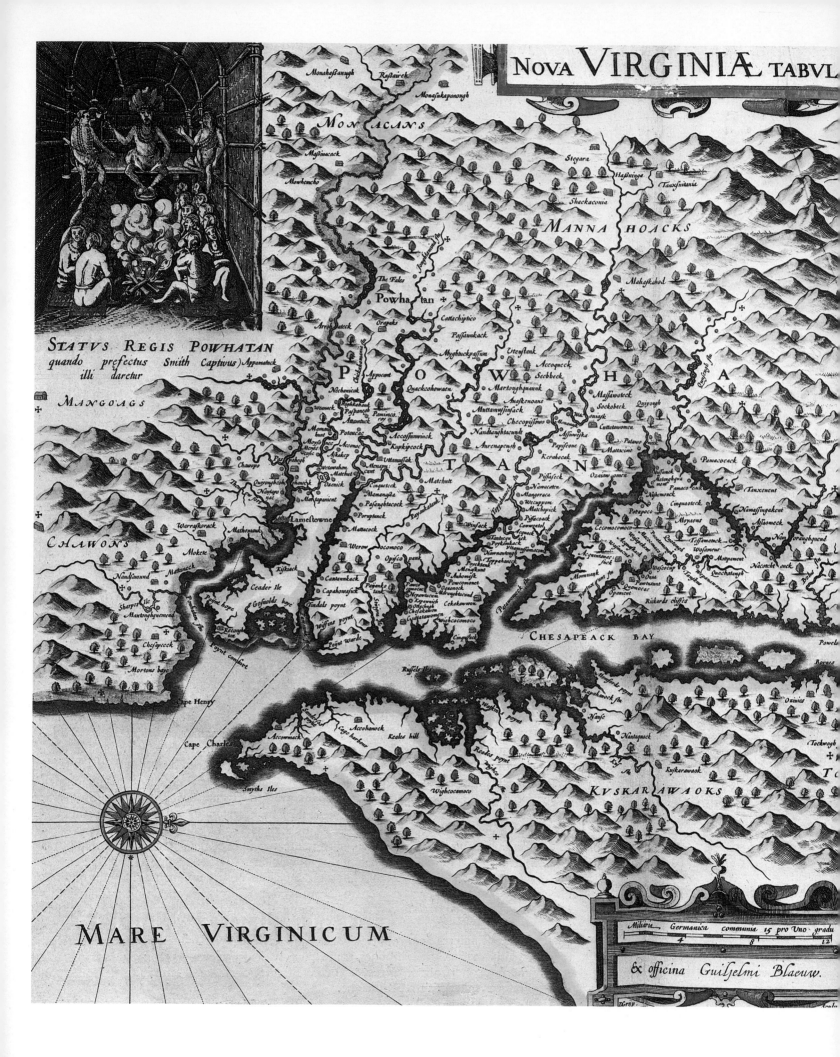

NOVA VIRGINIÆ TABVL

STATVS REGIS POWHATAN
quando prefectus Smith Captivus)
illi daretur Appamatuck

MONACANS

MANNA HOACKS

POWHATAN

MANGOAGS

CHAWONS

Powhatan

The Falls

James towne

CHESAPEACK BAY

Cape Henry

Cape Charles

Smyths Iles

KVSKARAWAOKS

MARE VIRGINICUM

& officina Guiljelmi Blaeuw.

Miliaria Germanica communia 15 pro Vno gradu

Map of Virginia in Willem Janszoon Blaeu's APPENDIX THEATRI A. ORTELII, (Amsterdam, 1631). Blaeu's map is derived from Captain John Smith's map of 1606.

The voice here, so informed with sensibility, belongs to the lone original inhabitant of the island: the semi-human Caliban, his name an anagram of *cannibal*. With man-like legs and fish-like arms, he is the freckled whelp littered by the foul witch Sycorax. Caliban worships a strange god, Setebos, the great devil of the Patagonians referred to in Richard Eden's *History of Travel*. The original cast-list of the First Folio describes Caliban as "a savage and deformed slave." He performs a slave's menial functions—making fires, fetching wood—for the island's stern but enlightened master, Prospero, who brings civilizing instruction. "When thou cam'st first," Caliban recalls to him,

> Thou strok'st me and made much of me, wouldst give me
> Water with berries in't, and teach me how
> To name the bigger light, and how the less,
> That burn by day and night; and then I lov'd thee,
> And show'd thee all the qualities o' th' isle,
> The fresh springs, brine-pits, barren place and fertile.

But nurture cannot alter nature, nor can it change the inevitable relationship between slave and master. Caliban's angry outburst—"You taught me language, and my profit on't / Is, I know how to curse"—expresses the despairing protest of all dispossessed peoples toward their colonial overlords. As demonstrated by the machinations of Antonio, restlessly thirsting after power, no less than by the firewater supplied to Caliban by Trinculo and Stephano, the Europeans bring corruption as well as higher civilization. *The Tempest,* moving profoundly on multiple levels, resonates with Shakespeare's prophetic vision of imperialism.

This page: *When Shakespeare has Othello speak of "men whose heads do grow beneath their shoulders," he is probably thinking of tall tales told by travelers in books such as THE VOYAGES AND TRAVAILES OF SIR JOHN MAUNDEVILE (London, 1583). Supposedly a travel guide to the Holy Land compiled in the fourteenth century, Mandeville's book describes marvels thought to exist in far-away eastern settings such as Persia and India. By Shakespeare's day it had become a folk classic, printed many times in various languages.*

Not surprisingly, travel literature furnished him with sources. Shakespeare drew upon pamphlet accounts of how Sir George Summers, on his way to Captain John Smith's Virginian colony aboard the *Sea-Adventure* in the summer of 1609, was separated by storm from the rest of the fleet and cast adrift in the Bermudas. There he and his men found web-footed fowl the size of English plovers, tortoises that provided "reasonable toothsome (some say) wholesome meat," and fresh water that gushed and softly bubbled before vanishing underground. Yet these were the dangerous and dreaded islands described by William Strachey in his *True Reportory of the Wrack,* islands that

> because they be so terrible to all that ever touched on them, and such tempests, thunders, and other fearful objects are seen and heard about them, that they be called commonly, The Devil's Islands, and are feared and avoided of all sea travellers alive, above any other place in the world. Yet it pleased our merciful God, to make even this hideous and hated place, both the place of our safety, and means of our deliverance.

Providentially, Strachey, Summers, and the rest returned to tell their story.

Providentially also, Shakespeare seems to have had access to Strachey's account, contained in a letter not published until a decade after the dramatist's death. But Shakespeare also consulted Sylvester Jourdain's *Discovery of the Bermudas* and the Council of Virginia's *True Declaration of the Estate of the Colony in Virginia, with a confutation of such scandalous reports as have tended to the disgrace of so worthy an enterprise,* both published in 1610, only a year before *The Tempest* was acted before James at Court. And Shakespeare's curious interest in the New World surfaces also in an otherwise puzzling small detail. The "burden" (or chorus) to Ariel's lovely song, "Come unto these yellow sands," goes "dispersedly," twice, "Bow-wow":

> Bow-wow.
> The watch dogs bark.
> Bow-wow.
> Hark, hark! I hear
> The strain of strutting chanticleer
> Cry, Cock-a-diddle-dow.

This burden, it seems, derives from James Rosier's account of a ceremonial Indian dance in the Virginia colony. "One among them, the eldest as he is judged, riseth right up, the others sitting still; and looking about, suddenly cries with a loud voice, *Baugh, Waugh*...the men altogether answering the same, fall a stamping round about the fire...with sundry outcries."

XVI.
A
DISCOVERY
OF THE BARMV-
DAS, OTHERWISE
called the Ile of
DIVELS:

By Sir THOMAS GATES, Sir
GEORGE SOMMERS, and Cap-
tayne NEWPORT, with
diuers others.

Set forth for the loue of my Country, and also for the good of the
Plantation in Virginia.

SIL. IOVRDAN.

LONDON,
Printed by *Iohn Windet,* and are to be fold by *Roger Barnes*
in S. *Dunstanes* Church-yard in Fleet-streete, vn-
der the Diall. 1610.

Opposite page, below: *In A DIS-COVERY OF THE BARMUDAS, OTHERWISE CALLED THE ILE OF DIVELS (London, 1610), Sylvester Jourdain tells the tale of a terrible storm that wrecked his ship on the coast of Bermuda. Jourdain's book is not only one of the earliest accounts of the Bermuda Triangle, but a source for the island setting and the storm in Shakespeare's THE TEMPEST.*

Below: *An Indian dance as depicted in Thomas Harriot's A BRIEFE AND TRUE REPORT OF THE NEW FOUND LAND OF VIRGINIA (Frankfurt-am-Main, 1590). In 1585 Harriot had been sent by Sir Walter Ralegh on a voyage to survey Virginia. Another member of the expedition, John White, made water-color drawings of Virginia and its natives, from which the engraved illustrations were copied.*

Solemn music sounds in *The Tempest*. Having united lovers and rendered foes impotent by his art, Prospero prepares to abjure his magic by breaking his staff and drowning his book. Biographers have found irresistible the temptation to identify the magus-protagonist of *The Tempest*—capable of bedimming the noontide sun and opening graves at his command—with the dramatic artificer who achieved similar miracles through his art. At least they used to find it irresistible, until a later generation of critics, recognizing the intrinsically public nature of theatre, drew back from ransacking the plays for clues to the interior life of their creator. Prospero is, after all, a character in a romance, not Shakespeare's alter ego. And besides, Shakespeare did not renounce the stage in *The Tempest* but returned for another bow two years later with his festive history of *Henry VIII*.

At last, under a Stuart, the Shakespeare who had complained in his Sonnets of art made tongue-tied by authority could dramatize a Tudor reign. But proximity still necessitated cosmetic surgery. The dramatist clears Henry of the warts with which history and his own nature had plentifully endowed him, and the play ends with Anne of the thousand days a happy mother rather than an executioner's victim. Contemplating the infant Elizabeth, richly swaddled in her christening mantle, Archbishop Cranmer prophesies wonders to come, first in the times of the maiden phoenix, then under the successor destined to rise starlike from her sacred ashes:

> Wherever the bright sun of heaven shall shine,
> His honour and the greatness of his name
> Shall be, and make new nations.

Possibly Cranmer here envisions the Virginia colonies of the Jacobean age. The original performance of *Henry VIII* never reached that moment of ecstatic consummation, however. Before the last act a spark from a discharging cannon—one of the play's numerous spectacular effects—lighted the overhead roof thatching, and in less than an hour the great Globe itself, along with an adjoining tenement, had been consumed to unsacred ashes, leaving not a rack behind. Miraculously, everybody managed to escape unscathed through the two narrow exits.

A year later a second Globe opened its doors on the same spot. This theatre, "said to be the fairest that ever was in England" (so Chamberlain breathlessly reported), stood until it was pulled down in 1644, when Civil War engulfed England and all theatrical activity had ceased.

Rebuilding proved costly, coming to perhaps twice the £700 or £800 originally estimated. The burden fell upon the shareholders obliged by the terms of their lease to "maintain and repair" the house. Shakespeare may well have decided, around this time, to retire from the profession he had served—as playwright, actor, and manager—for over two astonishing decades. An early biographer, Nicholas Rowe, reports on the final phase: "The latter part of his life was spent, as all men of good sense will wish theirs may be, in ease, retirement, and the conversation of friends. He had the good fortune to gather an estate equal to his occasion, and, in that, to his wish; and is said to have spent some years before his death at his native Stratford."

The material success that rewarded Shakespeare for his theatrical endeavors appealed to Victorian philistinism. "It is certain," smiled Samuel Smiles in his *Self-Help,* "that he prospered in his business, and realized sufficient to enable him to retire upon a competency to his native town of Stratford-upon-Avon." *He prospered in his business.* We shudder, understandably. The career sorts uncomfortably with our romantic stereotype of the poet. But then Shakespeare lived before the Romantic Age; fortunately, he did not suffer Keats's fate. Nor had the fatal division between high culture and popular culture yet taken place. In his own time Shakespeare achieved the status not of a literary classic but of the preeminent playwright of the preeminent theatrical company of the day. With the mundane rewards conferred by the applause of multitudes, he invested wisely in property, mainly in his native Stratford and environs.

In 1597 he had bought New Place, the five-gabled house of brick and timber, warmed by no fewer than ten fireplaces, that another successful Stratfordian, Sir Hugh Clopton (he had become Lord Mayor of London), built in the previous century. In May 1602, in nearby Old Stratford, Shakespeare purchased 107 acres of arable land, plus twenty acres of pasture, for the goodly sum of £320. Three years later he obtained, for £440, a half interest in a lease of tithes on corn, hay, and the like, which netted him £60 each year. Finally, in March 1613, he bought the Blackfriars Gatehouse in London, a dwelling built partly over "a great gate" abutting the street that led to Puddle Wharf, where water-taxis could transport him to the Bankside stage-land. The Gatehouse stood only a couple of hundred yards from the Blackfriars playhouse, the artificially illuminated indoor theatre which since 1609 had served as winter headquarters for the King's Men. The situation of the new property was thus convenient, but it apparently represented merely an investment on Shakespeare's part. In the conveyance he describes himself as "William Shakespeare of Stratford-upon-Avon in the county of Warwick, gentleman." The sojourner had returned from the teeming metropolis to his provincial roots.

One of the earliest maps of the New World in the Strassburg 1513 edition of Claudius Ptolomaeus's GEOGRAPHIE OPUS NOVISSIMA, based on the recent discoveries of Spanish and Portuguese explorers. It shows that with the exception of Florida, the Caribbean islands, and the north coast of South America, most of the western hemisphere was "terra incognita."

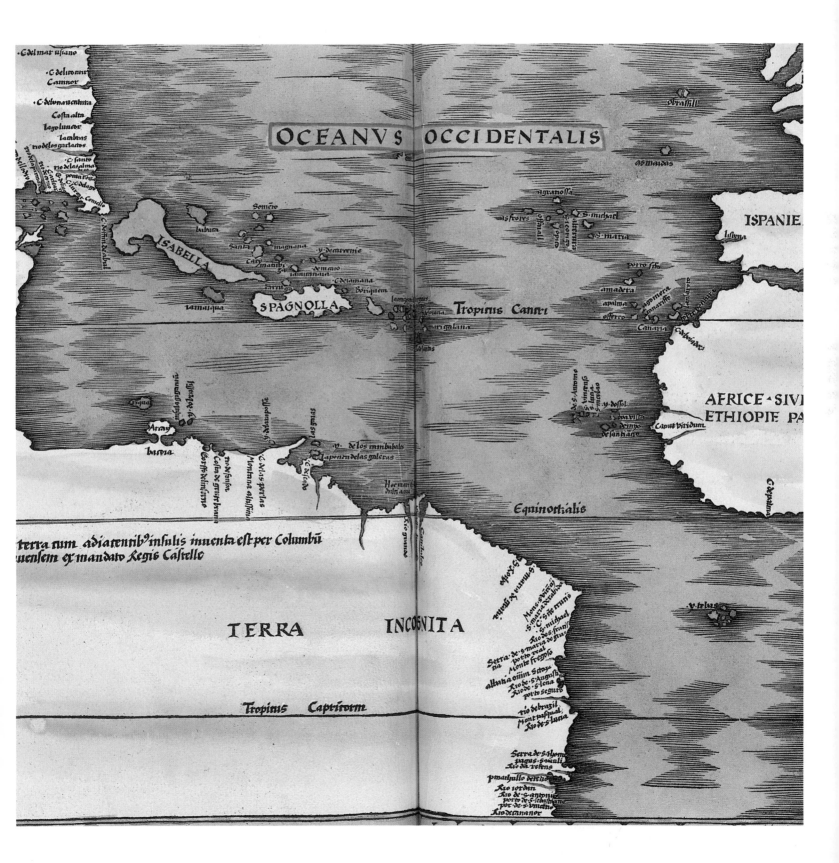

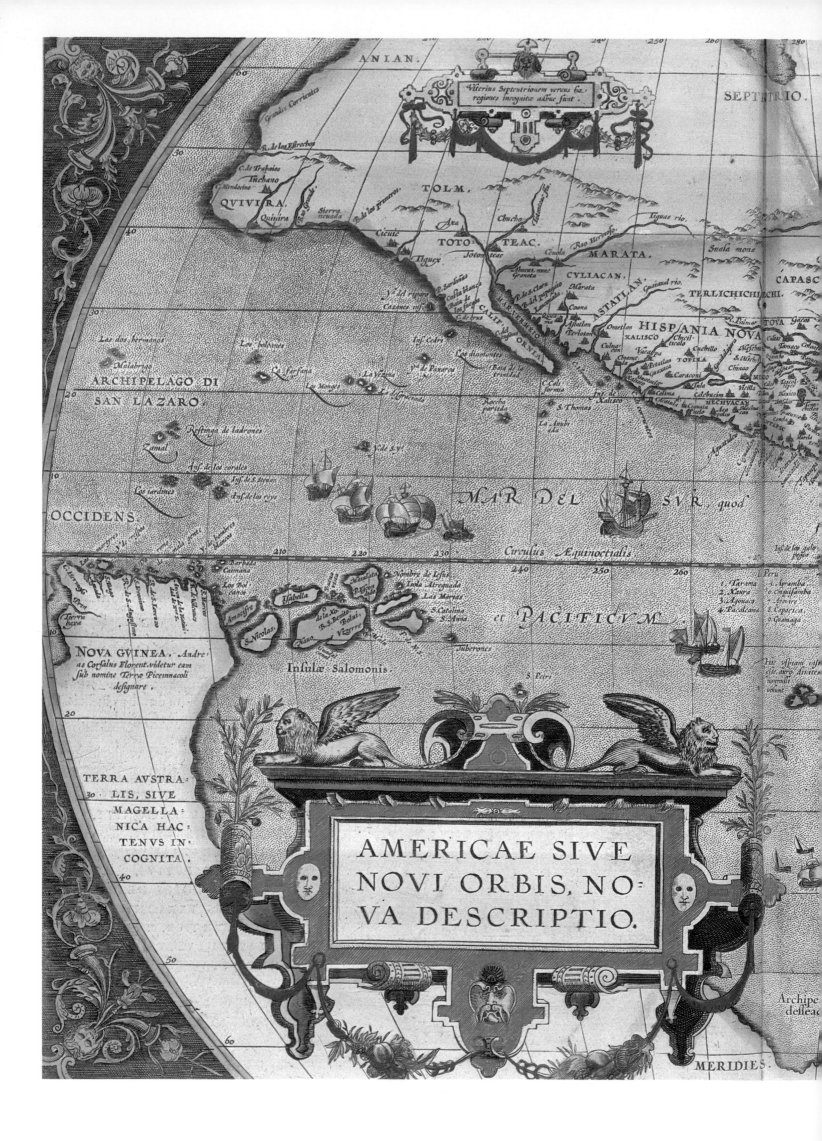

ANIAN.

SEPTENTRIO.

Vlterius Septentrionem versus hae regiones incognitae adhuc sunt.

Grandes Corrientes

R. de los Estrechos

C. de Trabaios
Tuchano
C. Mendocino
QVIVIRA.
Quivira

Rio Grande

Sierra neuada

TOLM.

Axa

Chucho

Tiguas rio.

Cicuie

TOTO: TEAC.

Tiguex

Jotontiteac

Acus

Rio Hermoso

Suala mons

Cenola

MARATA.

Y. del riparo

Costa blanca

Baia de los fuegos

P. de S. Clara
B. de S. paraiso
Lonedada

Abacus, nunc
Granata

CVLIACAN.

Macata

CAPASC

Cazanes inf.

C. de cruz

Coana

Astatlan.

Guazaul rio.

TERLICHICHIECHI.

Las dos hermanas

Malabrigo

Los boloñes

Y. farfana

Los Monges

Y. de Pxaros

La Vezina

Baia de la trinidad

Ometlan

Astatlan
Perlatan

Culiacan

HISPANIA NOVA

XALISCO

Chcil ticolo

Vacolpa

MECHVACAN

TOVA
Gacos

Colat

Tamaco
Colaat

ARCHIPELAGO DI

SAN LAZARO.

Inf. Cedri

Los diamantes

Baia de S. Christoforo

C. Cali formia

Inf. de Xalisco

Petatlan

TOPIRA

Guazacan

Caraconi

Tula

Colima

Calcbucim

Roccha partida

S. Thomas

La Amcbi dela

MVGO

Mechuacan

Restinga de ladrones

Zamal

Jde S. yf

MAR DEL SVR, quod

OCCIDENS.

Inf. de los corales

Inf. de S. Simon

Los iardines

Inf. de los reyes

Circulus Aequinoctialis

C. tierra firme

Barbada
Caimana

Los Dol canos

Ysabella

Amacifte

S. Nicolas.

de la Xo.
B. S. Benito
Bolui.
Naño

Matalate

Malagate

P. S. Spirito

Vzgero

Nombre de Iesus

Iola Atreguada

Las Marias

S. Catalina

S. Ania

240

et PACIFICVM.

250

260

1. Tarama
2. Xaura
3. Aguaco
4. Pacalcauna

5. Ayramba
6. Cuiquissamba
7. Axmey
8. Caparica
9. Guamaga

Tierra baxa

Tiberones

S. Petri

NOVA GVINEA, Andre: as Corsalus Florent. videtur eam sub nomine Terrae Piccennacoli designare.

Insulae Salomonis.

TERRA AVSTRA:
LIS, SIVE
MAGELLA:
NICA HAC:
TENVS IN:
COGNITA.

AMERICAE SIVE NOVI ORBIS, NOVA DESCRIPTIO.

MERIDIES.

Archipe
d'esflea

A map of the Americas from the London 1606 edition of Abraham Ortelius's atlas THEATRUM ORBIS TERRARUM, or "Theatre of the Whole World." This map, in comparison with the 1513 map in Ptolomaeus, is a reminder that Shakespeare lived in an exciting century of exploration, during which the magnitude of the New World was clearly defined.

This Indenture made

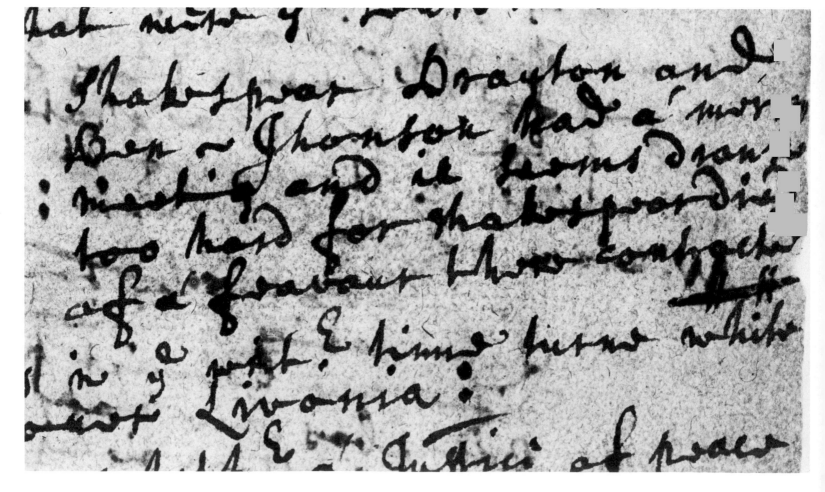

Shakespear Drayton and
Ben Jhonson had a merry
meeting and itt seems drank
too hard for Shakespear died
of a feavour there contracted
... in ye ... time hurne whic...
Livonia :
... Justice of peace

Opposite page, top: *Conveyance, or deed, to Shakespeare's London property in Blackfriars—purchased March 10, 1613, from Henry Walker. This is the rendee's or purchaser's copy which would have been kept by Shakespeare himself and therefore did not require his signature.*

Opposite page, bottom: *The diaries of John Ward, vicar of Stratford from 1662 to 1681, give information about Shakespeare that probably circulated as local gossip. This entry in the 1661-63 volume gives a report of Shakespeare's death.*

A half century following Shakespeare's burial in Holy Trinity Church, the vicar of Stratford, the Reverend John Ward, was still in touch with a living tradition, for he knew Shakespeare's younger daughter Judith in her old age. He refers to her as "Mrs. Queeny" (she had married Richard Quiney) in his notebooks. Ward confirms Rowe by recording that "Mr. Shakespeare... frequented the plays all his younger time, but in his elder days lived at Stratford." The vicar goes on to note that Shakespeare "supplied the stage with 2 plays every year, and for that had an allowance so large, that he spent at the rate of a £1,000 a year, as I have heard." The two plays a year do not strain credulity, but the £1,000 has all the earmarks of legendary exaggeration. Shakespeare's theatrical proceeds probably did not much exceed a fifth of that amount—a handsome income nonetheless, when a well-paid schoolmaster pulled down £20 a year. Ward's disclaimer, "as I have heard," testifies to the uncertain basis of his report.

So too he includes an exculpatory "it seems" in his note on how Shakespeare met his end: "Shakespeare, Drayton, and Ben Jonson had a merry meeting, and it seems drank too hard, for Shakespeare died of a fever there contracted." Ward's testimony—the only such rumor to come down—has a certain plausibility. The Warwickshire poet Michael Drayton, who had surveyed England's pleasant land in the hexameter couplets of his *Poly-Olbion,* stayed now and then in Clifford Chambers, only two miles south of Stratford. Jonson, whose thirst could do justice to a merry meeting, was on terms of familiar camaraderie (as well as rivalry) with Shakespeare. And the wedding of Judith Shakespeare two months before her father's decease furnished a likely enough occasion for conviviality.

In windswept March, Shakespeare summoned his solicitor for deathbed revisions to the will he had dictated early in the new year, when he could still describe himself (in conventional testamentary terms) as "in perfect health and memory." In what is arguably the most notorious bequest in literary history, he bequeathed to his wife the second-best bed. To his old comrades John Heminges, Richard Burbage, and Henry Condell—fellow actors and shareholders, all three with the King's Men—he left small sums for memorial rings. But Shakespeare's main concern was to keep the bulk of his estate intact for the anticipated male issue of his elder, and favorite, daughter Susanna. She was married to the respected Stratford physician John Hall. But she produced no male issue, and before the end of the century the dramatist's direct line had died out.

The library Shakespeare drew upon for his plays—Holinshed's *Chronicles,* North's Plutarch, and the rest—he fails to mention. Books would have been itemized separately in the inventory of his possessions, which has never surfaced. Nor does he allude to play manuscripts. The poet's will is the prosaic testament of a Jacobean man of substance, and as such would in due course fuel anti-Stratfordian fires. But of course wills usually are severely practical documents. Besides, the play scripts belonged to his troupe, and were probably stored at the Globe, where they had apparently escaped the conflagration that destroyed the first theatre of that name. That was on June 29, 1613. Informed accounts refer to the loss only of "a few forsaken cloaks." By contrast, the fire that took the Fortune theatre in 1621 deprived the actors of "all their apparel and playbooks."

Thirty-seven of Shakespeare's plays survive, thirty-eight if one includes *The Two Noble Kinsmen.* The author himself acted in some of them. Tradition holds that he played the Ghost in *Hamlet* and old Adam in *As You Like It*—dignified minor parts. Sometimes he acted in the plays of other writers. But Shakespeare mostly left the acting to others; so his productivity decreed. Even so, he must have composed rapidly. "His mind and hand went together," his awed friends from the King's Men report, "and what he thought, he uttered with that easiness, that we have scarce received from him a blot in his papers." Probably they exaggerated; we know that Shakespeare revised. But it is the general impression that counts.

He did well by his company, becoming their most applauded dramatist. But neither he nor they- could have forecast the judgment of posterity. That the BBC should decide to televise the whole enormous canon may at first glance seem a breathtaking gamble, but in a way it need not surprise us. Even the least cherished of the plays—*Love's Labor's Lost,* or *Pericles,* or any of half a dozen others—have a way of returning to the repertory and captivating viewers with their unexpected revelations. The theatrical history of Shakespeare's works, which has inspired numerous special studies and exhibitions, lies beyond the scope of the present survey. Here we must content ourselves with furnishing a select portfolio of illustrations to a half dozen of the plays. Let it suffice that these plays—*Romeo and Juliet, A Midsummer Night's Dream, Julius Caesar, Henry V, Hamlet,* and *Macbeth*—offer, by their diversity and richness of association, a representative microcosm of an achievement unparalleled in Western culture.

3

The
Play's
The
Thing

Suit the action to the word, the word to the action; with this special observance, that you o'erstep not the modesty of nature; for anything so o'erdone is from the purpose of playing, whose end, both at the first and now, was and is, to hold, as 'twere, the mirror up to nature; to show virtue her own feature, scorn her own image, and the very age and body of the time his form and pressure.

THE GLOBE PLAYHOUSE. This famous scale model of Shakespeare's Globe (lent to the Folger by the Trustees of Hofstra College) was completed by John Cranford Adams, with the assistance of Irwin Smith, in 1954. Inevitably, in view of the unavailability of any authenticated contemporary sketch of the interior of the Globe, particular details must be hypothesized from such evidence as the De Witt sketch of the rival Swan playhouse. It is not surprising, therefore, that many recent investigators differ in some respects from Adams's reconstruction of the interior (doubting, for example, that there was a small proscenium-arch inner stage at the rear of the thrust stage of the Globe). There is room for some doubt, also, as to whether the Globe was polygonal (as depicted by Visscher and as shown in the Adams model) or round (as the Hollar view would suggest). See the discussion on pages 88–95.

Romeo and Juliet

Two households, both alike in dignity,
In fair Verona, where we lay our scene,
From ancient grudge break to new mutiny,
Where civil blood makes civil hands unclean.
From forth the fatal loins of these two foes
A pair of star-cross'd lovers take their life;
Whose misadventur'd piteous overthrows
Doth with their death bury their parents' strife.
The fearful passage of their death-mark'd love,
And the continuance of their parents' rage,
Which, but their children's end, nought could remove,
Is now the two hours' traffic of our stage;
The which if you with patient ears attend,
What here shall miss, our toil shall strive to mend.

Opposite page: *Marcia Haydée and Richard Cragun of the Stuttgart Ballet, performing Sergei Prokofiev's* ROMEO AND JULIET.
This page: **1** *Two figures in rich Italian costume tread the measures of a dance that might have been performed at the Capulets' ball in* ROMEO AND JULIET; *from* IL BALLARINO *(Venice, 1581) by Fabrizio Caroso.* **2** *Title-page woodcut of Romeo Montecchi and Giulietta Capelletti, the lovers in an early Italian forerunner of Shakespeare's* ROMEO AND JULIET, *Luigi da Porto's* NOVELLA NOVAMENTE RITROVATA D'UNA INNAMORAMENTO *(Venice, 1535).* **3** *Title page of the good Second Quarto of Shakespeare's play (London, 1599).* **4** *Dueling techniques, as illustrated in* VINCENTIO SAVIOLO, HIS PRACTISE *(London, 1595), a translation of a 1558 treatise that would have been informative not only for Elizabethan gentlemen but also for actors preparing stage duels such as that between Tybalt and Mercutio.*

1

2

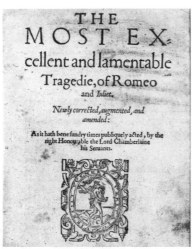

3

4

1 *A gentlewoman of Verona, as depicted in Pietro Bertelli's costume book, DIVERSARUM NATIONUM HABITUS (Padua, 1594).* 2 *Edna May Oliver as the Nurse in George Cukor's 1936 MGM film of ROMEO AND JULIET; watercolor sketch by Dan Sayre Grossbeck. Two famous Juliets,* 3 *Julia Marlowe, ca. 1887, and* 4 *Ellen Terry, 1882. Playbill* 5 *and 1759 engraving* 6 *of Spranger Barry and Isabella Nossiter in a Covent Garden production. Two more well-known Juliets,*

7 *opera star Nellie Melba, ca. 1896, and* 8 *Fanny Kemble, ca. 1830. Engraving* 9 *and playbill* 10 *of David Garrick's 1753 Romeo at Theatre Royal in Drury Lane.* 11 *Renaissance ballroom scene, from NIEUWEN IEUCHT SPIEGHEL (Netherlands, ca. 1620).* 12 *Romeo (Richard Cragun) hiding behind mask as Tybalt looks on: Capulets' ball as enacted by the Stuttgart Ballet, 1979.* 13 *Leslie Howard and Norma Shearer in the 1936 MGM film of ROMEO AND*

JULIET. **14** *The Cushman sisters, Charlotte and Susan, as Romeo and Juliet, 1846.* **15** *Leonard Whiting and Olivia Hussey in Franco Zeffirelli's 1968 film.* **16** *Carol Lawrence and Larry Kert in the 1960 Broadway production of WEST SIDE STORY, a modern musical adaptation of ROMEO AND JULIET, with music by Leonard Bernstein and lyrics by Stephen Sondheim.* **17** *Henry Fuseli's painting (1809) of Romeo slaying Paris at Juliet's bier.*

14

15

13

16

17

Midsummer Night's Dream

THESEUS. More strange than true. I never may believe
These antique fables, nor these fairy toys.
Lovers and madmen have such seething brains,
Such shaping fantasies, that apprehend
More than cool reason ever comprehends.

. . . . .

HIPPOLYTA. But all the story of the night told over,
And all their minds transfigur'd so together,
More witnesseth than fancy's images,
And grows to something of great constancy,
But howsoever strange and admirable.

Opposite page: *Arthur Rackham's water-color and ink painting (1908) of The Wedding Scene in A MIDSUMMER NIGHT'S DREAM.*
This page: **1** *"Oberyon," an antecedent of Shakespeare's Oberon, in a manuscript BOOK OF MAGIC dating from ca. 1580.* **2** *Illustration from ROBIN GOOD-FELLOW, HIS MAD PRANKES AND MERRY JESTS (London, 1639).* **3** *Title page of the good First Quarto of A MID-SOMMER NIGHTS DREAME (London, 1600).* **4** *Page from a Renaissance edition (Venice, 1538) of Ovid's METAMOR-PHOSES, showing the tragic outcome of the Pyramus and Thisbe story, a remote source of ROMEO AND JULIET and the subject of the Mechanicals' play in A MIDSUMMER NIGHT'S DREAM.*

1

2

3

4

1

2

3

5

6

7

8

4

1 *Autograph manuscript of composer Felix Mendelssohn's overture to A MID-SUMMER NIGHT'S DREAM, arranged for two performers (July 10, 1826).* **2, 3** *Bottom with the Fairies; two costume sketches from Charles Kean's scrapbook for a production such as that announced in the Princess's Theatre program*

4 *shown below. Program* **5** *and scene* **6** *from Max Reinhardt's 1935 Warner Bros. film, with James Cagney as Bottom and Anita Louise as Titania.* **7** *Poet-painter William Blake's oval watercolor of Oberon and Titania (ca. 1790).* **8** *Titania and Bottom; lithograph from latter half of the nineteenth century by*

Currier and Ives. **9** *Scene from LE SONGE D'UNE NUIT D'ÉTÉ, Jirí Trnka's 1959 Czechoslovakian marionette film.* **10** *Titania and Bottom, as depicted by Henry Fuseli, 1794. Puck, as depicted by* **11** *Arthur Rackham (1908) and* **12** *Henry Fuseli (ca. 1790).*

9

10

11

12

Julius Caesar

CASSIUS. Why, he that cuts off twenty years of life
Cuts off so many years of fearing death.
BRUTUS. Grant that, and then is death a benefit.
So are we Caesar's friends, that have abridg'd
His time of fearing death. Stoop, Romans, stoop,
And let us bathe our hands in Caesar's blood
Up to the elbows, and besmear our swords.
Then walk we forth, even to the market-place,
And waving our red weapons o'er our heads,
Let's all cry 'Peace, freedom, and liberty!'
CASSIUS. Stoop then, and wash. How many ages hence
Shall this our lofty scene be acted over
In states unborn and accents yet unknown!

Opposite page: *BRUTUS AND THE GHOST OF CAESAR, engraving by Edward Scriven from painting by R. Westall (London, 1802).*
This page: **1** *Woodcut medallion of Caesar from "The Life of Julius Caesar" in Thomas North's edition (London, 1579) of Plutarch's "Parallel Lives" or LIVES OF THE NOBLE GRECIANS AND ROMANES COMPARED, the principal source for* Shakespeare's JULIUS CAESAR. **2** *Two-page spread from C. Julius Caesar's COMMENTARII (Lausanne, 1571), a Renaissance Latin edition of Caesar's COMMENTARIES on the Gallic Wars.* **3** *Map of Rome from TOPOGRAPHIA ROMAE CUM TABULIS GEOGRAPHIS (Frankfurt, 1627), by Jean Jacques Boissard and others.*

1

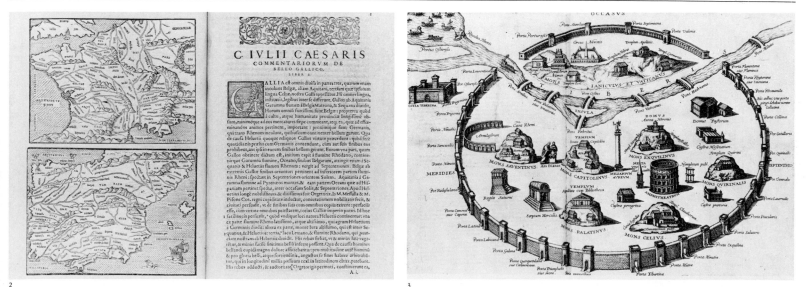

2

3

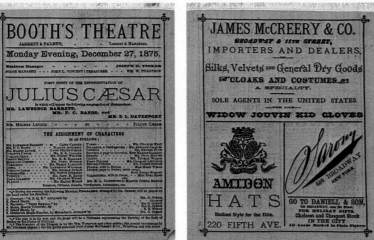

1

2

3

4

5

1, 2 *Front and back of a playbill printed on silk for the 1875 Jarrett and Palmer production of JULIUS CAESAR in New York.* 3 *Scene from Joseph Mankiewicz's 1953 MGM film of JULIUS CAESAR starring Marlon Brando as Mark Antony and James Mason as Brutus.* 4 *Program for 1977 National Theatre production in London with Sir John Gielgud as Julius Caesar.* 5 *Frederick Tyrone Power as Brutus (ca. 1913).* 6 *Playbill for an 1864 Booth Benefit at New York's Winter Garden featuring the three Booth brothers, Edwin, Junius Brutus, Jr., and John Wilkes.* 7 *Engraving of the post-assassi-* nation scene from Nicholas Rowe's 1709 edition of Shakespeare's works. 8 *Brutus (Richard Pasco) over the slain Caesar (Charles Gray) in the 1978 BBC Television production for THE SHAKESPEARE PLAYS.* 9 *Profile of Caesar from Guillaume du Choul's DISCOURS DE LA RELIGION DES ANCIENS ROMAINS (Lyon, 1556).* 10 *Profile of Caesar from program of The Players' Sixth Annual Classic Revival in New York (1927).* 11 *Brutus falling on his sword, an engraving from Geoffrey Whitney's A CHOICE OF EMBLEMES (London, 1586).* 12 *Program for Joseph Mankiewicz's*

9

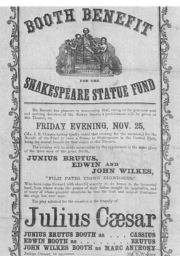

6

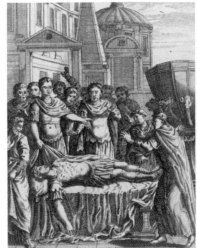

7

8

1953 MGM film. **13** *Cassius brooding, as depicted in program of 1927 Players' production.* **14** *Political cartoon by C. K. Berryman, showing William Howard Taft (as Julius Caesar) refusing appointment to the Supreme Court by President Theodore Roosevelt.* **15** *Boston Theatre playbill for an 1870 production.* **16** *Woodcut illustrating one of the prodigies preceding Caesar's assassination, from Julius Obsequens,* PRODIGIORUM LIBER *(Basel, 1552).* **17** *Poster promoting Olympic Theatre production by Edmund Tearle and Company, 1892.*

11

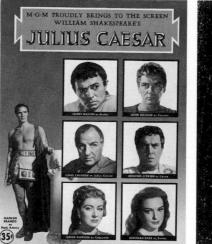

12

13

10

14

15

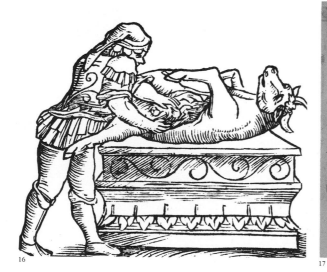

16

17

Henry V

O for a Muse of fire, that would ascend
The brightest heaven of invention,
A kingdom for a stage, princes to act,
And monarchs to behold the swelling scene!
Then should the warlike Harry, like himself,
Assume the port of Mars; and at his heels,
Leash'd in like hounds, should famine, sword, and fire,
Crouch for employment. But pardon, gentles all,
The flat unraised spirits that hath dar'd
On this unworthy scaffold to bring forth
So great an object. Can this cockpit hold
The vasty fields of France? Or may we cram
Within this wooden O the very casques
That did affright the air at Agincourt?

Opposite page: *Laurence Olivier in the title role of his celebrated 1944 film of HENRY V.*
Below: **1** *English bowman, from William Neade's THE DOUBLE ARMED MAN* (London, 1625). **2** *Renaissance cannon, as depicted by Albrecht Dürer in ETLICHE UNDERRICHT, ZU BEFESTIGUNG DER STETT (Nuremberg, 1527).*

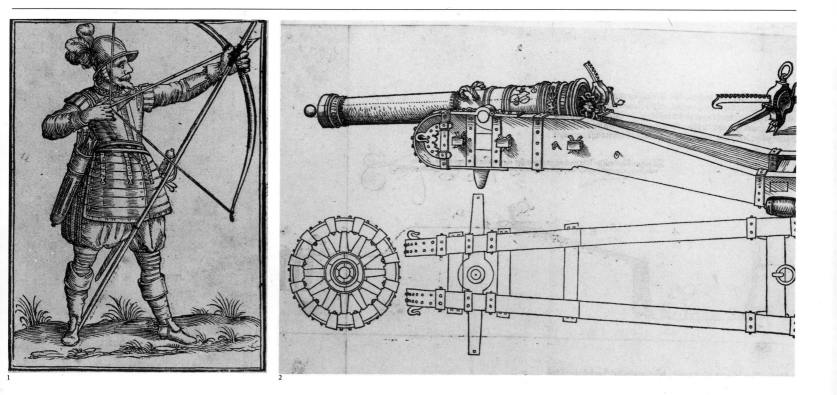

1

2

Photograph 1 and crayon drawing by Jackson F. Ernest 2 of Lewis Waller as Henry V (1905). 3 Charles Kemble as Henry V (1821). 4 Portrait of historical Henry V, from an engraving by Renold Elstracke (London, 1618). 5 Arms of Henry V, from Sir William Segar's NAMES AND ARMS OF THE KNIGHTS OF THE GARTER, a manuscript dating from 1606. 6 Illustration from Flavius Vegetius Renatus's DU FAIT DE GUERRE (Paris, 1536). 7 Frederick Thorne as Fluellen, in the 1876 Jarrett and Palmer production at Booth's Theatre in New York. 8 Cat carrying fire-bomb; hand-colored illustration from a 1607 German artillery manual, EIN WAHRES PRO-BIERTES UND PRACKTISCHES GESCHRIEBENES FEUERBUCH. 9 A military drill demonstrated in A BREIFE BOOKE UNTO PRIVATE CAPTAYNES, a 1562 manuscript by Henry Barrett.

1

3

5

2

4

6

7

8

9

11

10 *"The Siege of a Fortress"; woodcut by Albrecht Dürer, in ETLICHE UNDER-RICHT, ZU BEFESTIGUNG DER STETT (1527).* 11 *Henry V on horseback; costume designed for Charles Kean's 1859 Princess's Theatre production.* 12 *French army portrayed as war machine; from Michael Kahn's 1969 production of HENRY V at the American Shakespeare Theatre in Stratford, Connecticut.* 13 *Wedding scene from 1958 Old Vic production, with Laurence Harvey as Henry V.* 14 *Autographed shooting script for 1944 film of HENRY V directed by and starring Laurence Olivier.* 15 *GOD FOR HARRY, an original ink drawing by Byam Shaw, ca. 1900.* 16 *Poster from 1975 Royal Shakespeare Company production starring Alan Howard.* 17 *Poster from 1976 New York Shakespeare Festival production.*

10

12

14

16

13

15

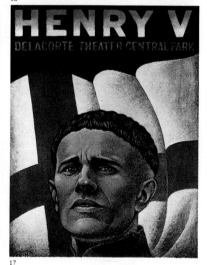

17

John Barrymore
1922

Hamlet

I have of late—but wherefore I know not—lost all my mirth, foregone all custom of exercises; and indeed it goes so heavily with my disposition that this goodly frame, the earth, seems to me a sterile promontory; this most excellent canopy the air, look you, this brave o'er-hanging firmament, this majestical roof fretted with golden fire—why, it appeareth no other thing to me than a foul and pestilent congregation of vapours. What a piece of work is a man! How noble in reason! how infinite in faculties! in form and moving, how express and admirable! in action, how like an angel! in apprehension, how like a god! the beauty of the world! the paragon of animals! And yet, to me, what is this quintessence of dust?

Opposite page: *Autographed photograph of John Barrymore as Hamlet, 1922.* **1** *View of Kronborg Castle, Elsinore; hand-colored engraving by Georg Braun (Cologne, ca. 1590).* **2** *Title page from DANORUM REGUM HEROUMQUE HISTORIE (Paris, 1514) by the Danish historian Saxo Grammaticus, a major source of the Hamlet story.* *Two important background books,* **3** *OF GHOSTES AND SPIRITES WALKING BY NYGHT, translated by Robert Harrison (London, 1572) from a Latin treatise by Ludwig Lavater, and* **4** *A TREATISE OF MELANCHOLIE (London, 1586) by Timothy Bright.* **5** *Title page of the 1604 good Second Quarto of HAMLET.*

1 *Edward Gordon Craig's stylized wood-cut of Hamlet for the Cranach Presse edition of the play (Weimar, 1928). Famous performers who have distinguished themselves in the role of Hamlet:* 2 *John Howard Payne, 1813;* 3 *Thomas Betterton, ca. 1661;* 4 *Maurice Evans, 1938;* 5 *H. Beerbohm Tree, ca. 1892;* 6 *Asta Nielsen, 1920;* 7 *Richard Burton, 1964;* 8 *Fritz Leiber, ca. 1920;* 9 *Henry Irving, 1888;* 10 *David Garrick, ca. 1754;* 11 *Edmund Kean, ca. 1814;* 12 *John Gielgud, 1939;* 13 *E. H. Sothern, ca. 1899;* 14 *Charles Kean, 1838; and* 15 *Colin Keith-Johnston, 1920s. Two of the most widely acclaimed Hamlets of the last century and a half,* 16 *Laurence Olivier (from the 1948 film) and* 17 *Edwin Booth (as*

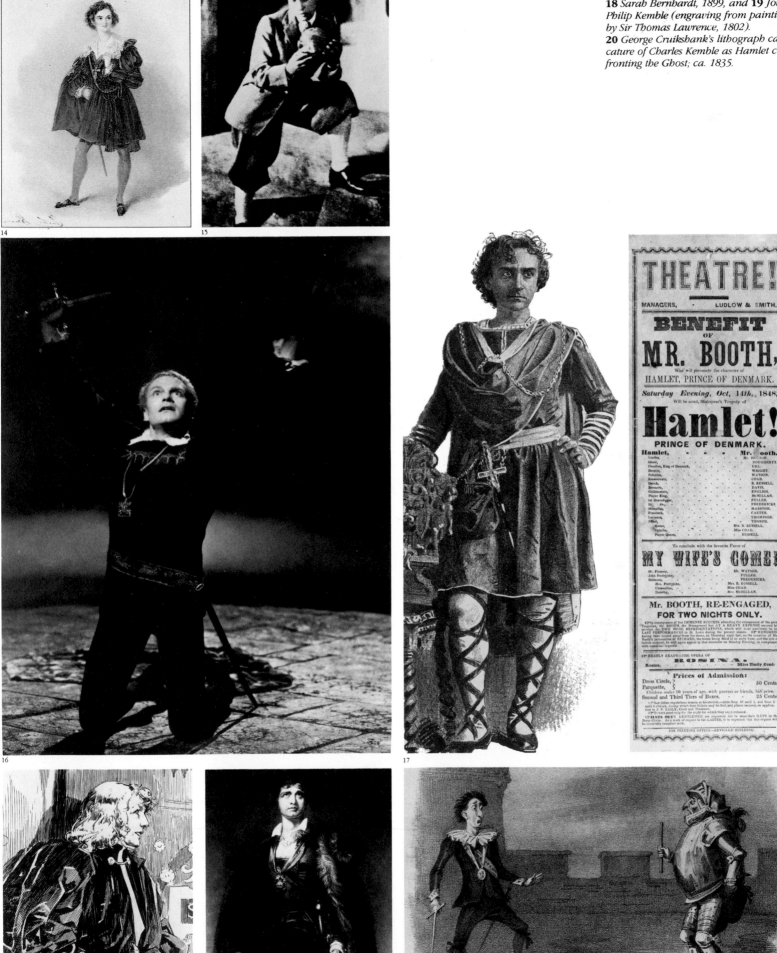

engraved by H. A. Thomas, ca. 1870).
18 *Sarah Bernhardt, 1899, and* **19** *John Philip Kemble (engraving from painting by Sir Thomas Lawrence, 1802).*
20 *George Cruikshank's lithograph caricature of Charles Kemble as Hamlet confronting the Ghost; ca. 1835.*

Macbeth

MACBETH....
How does your patient, doctor?
DOCTOR. Not so sick, my lord,
As she is troubled with thick-coming fancies
That keep her from her rest.
MACBETH. Cure her of that.
Canst thou not minister to a mind diseas'd,
Pluck from the memory a rooted sorrow,
Raze out the written troubles of the brain,
And with some sweet oblivious antidote
Cleanse the stuff'd bosom of that perilous stuff
Which weighs upon the heart?
DOCTOR. Therein the patient
Must minister to himself.
MACBETH. Throw physic to the dogs—I'll none of it.

Opposite page: George Romney's oil painting of Macbeth's meeting with the Witches (ca. 1780).
Below: 1 Genealogical tree showing King James's descent from Banquo; from John Leslie's DE ORIGINE, MORIBUS ET REBUS GESTIS SCOTORUM LIBRI DECEM (Rome, 1578). 2 King James's book on DAEMONOLOGIE (Edinburgh, 1597). 3 Illustration from title page of Matthew Hopkins's THE DISCOVERY OF WITCHES (London, 1647).

1

2

3

1 *Sleepwalking scene of Lady Macbeth, as engraved by Francois Gravelot from an ink and wash drawing by Francis Hayman for Thomas Hanmer's 1743–44 edition of Shakespeare.* **2** *Henry Fuseli's oil painting of MACBETH IN THE WITCHES' CAVE (1793). Three famous Lady Macbeths:* **3** *Kate Bateman as caricatured in 1875,* **4** *Charlotte Cushman,*

ca. 1860, and **5** Mrs. D. P. Bowers, ca. 1870. **6** Macbeth and Banquo meeting the Three Witches; engraving in the 1577 first edition of Shakespeare's principal source for the play, Raphael Holinshed's *CHRONICLES OF ENGLANDE, SCOTLANDE AND IRELANDE.* **7** Maurice Evans and Judith Anderson as Macbeth and Lady Macbeth (1942). **8** Mary Ann Yates as Lady Macbeth, 1769. Four more well-known Lady Macbeths: **9** Viola Allen ca. 1915, **10** Sarah Siddons, ante-1812, **11** Ellen Terry, ca. 1888, and **12** Julia Marlowe, ca. 1910. **13** Caricature of Henry Irving as Macbeth, ca. 1888. **14** Boydell engraving of Henry Fuseli's painting of Lady Macbeth entering with a taper (1803).

7

8

9

10

11

12

13

14

A CATALOGVE

of the feuerall Comedies, Hiftories, and Tragedies contained in this Volume.

COMEDIES.

HISTORIES.

TRAGEDIES.

It had been a thing, we confess, worthy to have been wished, that the Author himself had lived to have set forth and overseen his own writings. But since it hath been ordained otherwise, and he by death departed from that right, we pray you do not envy his friends the office of their care and pain to have collected and published them, and so to have published them, as where before you were abused with diverse stolen and surreptitious copies, maimed and deformed by the frauds and stealths of injurious impostors that exposed them, even those are now offered to your view cured, and perfect of their limbs; and all the rest, absolute in their numbers, as he conceived them. Who, as he was a happy imitator of Nature, was a most gentle expresser of it. His mind and hand went together. And what he thought, he uttered with that easiness, that we have scarce received from him a blot in his papers. But it is not our province, who only gather his works, and give them you, to praise him. It is yours that read him. And there we hope, to your divers capacities, you will find enough both to draw and hold you. For his wit can no more lie hid than it could be lost. Read him, therefore, and again, and again.

*From John Heminges and Henry Condell's First Folio
preface "To the great Variety of Readers"*

*Table of Contents listing the plays printed
in the First Folio of 1623. Owing to a delay
in its inclusion in the book, one play,
TROILUS AND CRESSIDA, was omitted
from the "Catalogue of the severall Comedies, Histories, and Tragedies contained
in this Volume."*

Half of Shakespeare's plays remained unpublished when their creator was laid to rest. His greatest playwriting contemporary did not display a similar benign neglect toward his literary progeny. In the year of Shakespeare's death, Ben Jonson brought together his own plays, masques, and incidental poetry in a splendid folio. Four years in the making, the thousand-page volume was published by one of the most reputable stationers of the day, William Stansby, commended by the English traveler Thomas Coryat from the Court of the Great Mogul as one of the "lovers of virtue and literature." At the top of the engraved emblematic title page of the 1616 folio stands Tragicomedy, equipped with her tragic crown and scepter but wearing the comic sock. Diminutive figures of Bacchus (with ivy-covered thyrsus) and ray-crowned Apollo (holding his lyre) flank her. Below, a satyr and shepherd—symbolizing satire and pastoral—play reed and pipe on either side of a classic amphitheatre. Beneath them the stately figures of Tragedy and Comedy stand in pillared niches. Tragedy wears the buskin; Comedy, the sock. Behind Tragedy an embroidered curtain stretches, while Comedy makes do with a plain cloth. Appropriate masks are fixed to the adjoining pillars. Thus framed, the title reads *The Works of Benjamin Jonson.*

It provoked derisive comment. "Pray tell me, Ben," a wit demanded,

> where doth the mystery lurk,
> What others call a play, you call a work.

To which, according to the epigram,

> The author's friend thus for the author says,
> "Ben's plays are works, when others' works are plays."

In appended cast-lists Jonson includes Shakespeare among the actors of *Every Man in His Humour* and *Sejanus.* The Jonson folio therefore furnishes its biographical crumbs. But, more important, it established a fateful precedent. Secure in the egoism which persuaded him that his plays were such as other plays should be, Jonson was the first Elizabethan dramatist to assemble his works in a collected edition. In a sense he made possible the Shakespeare Folio.

Very likely spurred on by the impact of the Jonson volume, a couple of stationers—William Jaggard and Thomas Pavier—set about publishing a collected Shakespeare in small individual volumes. That was in 1619. But after five plays had appeared, the Lord Chamberlain (no doubt acting on behalf of the King's Men) intervened to prohibit further unauthorized publication. Cunningly, before throwing in the sponge, Jaggard went on to issue five more plays with title pages antedated. The stage was now set for the First Folio of 1623.

To the Reader.

This Figure, that thou here seest put,
    It was for gentle Shakespeare cut;
Wherein the Grauer had a strife
    with Nature, to out-doo the life :
O, could he but haue drawne his wit
    As well in brasse, as he hath hit
Hisface ; the Print would then surpasse
    All, that vvas euer vvrit in brasse.
But, since he cannot, Reader, looke
    Not on his Picture, but his Booke.

                  B. I.

Mr. WILLIAM
SHAKESPEARES
COMEDIES,
HISTORIES, &
TRAGEDIES.

Published according to the True Originall Copies.

Martin Droeshout sculpsit London.

LONDON
Printed by Isaac Iaggard, and Ed. Blount. 1623.

Never did circumstances attach more prophetic significance to the appearance of a book, at least on the belletristic side. Some of the plays printed during Shakespeare's lifetime had appeared in appallingly corrupt texts, which the authorities have come to term Bad Quartos. *The Contention Betwixt the Two Famous Houses of York and Lancaster* and *The True Tragedy of Richard, Duke of York* diverge so dramatically from the authentic versions, for example, that centuries elapsed before scholars were able to determine conclusively—or almost conclusively—that these were in fact Bad Quartos of *2* and *3 Henry VI.* Another play, *The Taming of a Shrew* (printed in 1594), still enjoys an ambiguous status, the authorities being divided as to whether it served as Shakespeare's source for *The Taming of the Shrew* or represents a deformed version of that comedy. The 1603 First Quarto of *Hamlet* illustrates the problem. Here, in language worthy of the Duke in *Huckleberry Finn,* is the Prince pondering the great issue of whether life is worth enduring:

> To be or not to be, ay, there's the point,
> To die, to sleep, is that all? Ay, all:
> No, to sleep, to dream, ay, marry there it goes,
> For in that dream of death, when we awake,
> And borne before an everlasting judge,
> From whence no passenger ever returned,
> The undiscovered country at whose sight
> The happy smile, and the accursed damned....

Another, much better edition—this text authorized by the company—followed on the heels of the first, but even this Second Quarto presents many problems. One of Shakespeare's masterpieces, *Othello,* was not published separately until six years after the playwright's death. He had himself seen none of his plays through the press.

Posterity rejoices that the friends Shakespeare had remembered in his will chose to remember him. In 1623 Heminges and Condell, still active members of the King's Men, brought together the comedies, histories, and tragedies in the second great dramatic folio of the age. This volume they dedicated to the Earls of Pembroke and Montgomery, who had (the editors avouch) applauded these trifles on the stage, and shown their author, while he lived, many signs of favor. They go on to explain the pious considerations moving them to print the

plays. "We have but collected them," they write, "and done an office to the dead, to procure his orphans guardians; without ambition either of self-profit or fame: only to keep the memory of so worthy a friend and fellow alive, as was our Shakespeare." In another epistle, addressed "To the great Variety of Readers," they describe with awe the facility of the writer they commemorate: "His mind and hand went together, and what he thought he uttered with that easiness that we have scarce received from him a blot in his papers." To this claim irascible Ben retorted, "Would he had blotted a thousand!"—at the same time owning, however, that he "loved the man," and did "honor his memory (on this side idolatry) as much as any." But of course Heminges and Condell exaggerate; the texts of the plays themselves betray evidences of authorial second thoughts. In common with other great writers Shakespeare confronted (in Henry James's phrase) "the terrified revise." But never mind. The fecundity of the creative force that astonished and delighted his fellows speaks for itself on every page.

A consortium of stationers undertook the First Folio, but the actual printing progressed in the shop of William Jaggard and his son Isaac at the sign of the Half-Eagle and Key in Barbican. The elder Jaggard, who had for some time been blind and ill, died in 1623, as the book was being completed. Isaac probably supervised the last stages of the project, and his name appears on the title page along with that of Edward Blount, who was not a printer but a bookseller-sponsor of the venture. An early presentation copy, inscribed as from William Jaggard, is in the Folger Library, which possesses seventy-eight other copies: by far the largest collection of First Folios in the world. As these exemplars differ from one another in minute particulars, the value of multiple copies for editors faced with the task of establishing the text is manifest.

Martin Droeshout's engraved portrait on the title page is one of only two verified likenesses of Shakespeare, the other being the bust in the Stratford monument. Droeshout, who was only fifteen when Shakespeare died, presumably did not know his subject personally. His oddly proportioned handiwork is less than inspiring, and one does well to follow Jonson's advice to the reader: "look / Not on his picture, but his book."

That book contains thirty-six plays. Those printed for the

EDWARD GWYNN

M. VVilliam Shake-fpeare,

HIS

True Chronicle Hiftory of the life
and death of King *Lear*, and his
three Daughters.

With the vnfortunate life of E D G A R,
sonne and heire to the Earle of *Glocefter*, and
his fullen and affumed humour of T O M
of Bedlam.

*As it was plaid before the Kings Maiefty at White-Hall, vp-
pon S. Stephens night, in Chriftmas Hollidaies.*

By his Maiefties Seruants, playing vfually at the
Globe on the *Banck-fide.*

Printed for *Nathaniel Butter.*
1608.

The moft excellent Tragedie,

Rom: Nay thats not fo. *Mer:* I meane fir in delay,
We burne our lights by night, like Lampes by day,
Take our good meaning for our iudgement fits
Three times a day,ere once in her right wits.
Rom: So we meane well by going to this maske:
But tis no wit to goe.
Mer: Why *Romeo* may one aske?
Rom: I dreamt a dreame to night.
Mer: And fo did I, *Rom:* Why what was yours?
Mer: That dreamers often lie.
Rom: In bed a fleepe while they doe dreame things
Mer: Ah then I fee Queene Mab hath bin with you.
Ben: Queene Mab whats fhe?
She is the Fairies Midwife and doth come
In fhape no bigger than an Aggat ftone
On the forefinger of a Burgomafter,
Drawne with a teeme of little Atomi,
Athwart mens nofes when they lie a fleepe,
Her waggon fpokes are made of fpinners webs,
The couer, of the winges of Grafhoppers,
The traces are the Moone-fhine watrie beames,
The collers crickets bones,the lafh of filmes,
Her waggoner is a fmall gray coated flie,
Not halfe fo big as is a little worme,
Pickt from the lafie finger of a maide,
And in this fort fhe gallops vp and downe
Through Louers braines,and then they dream of loue
O're Courtiers knees:who ftrait on curfies dreame
O're Ladies lips,who dreame on kiffes ftrait:
Which oft the angrie Mab with blifters plagues,
Becaufe their breathes with fweet meats tainted are:
Sometimes fhe gallops ore a Lawers lap,
                                                   And

of Romeo and Iuliet.

Fiue times in that,ere once in our fine wits.
Ro. And we meane well in going to this Mask,
But tis no wit to go.
Mer. Why, may one a ke?
Rom. I dreampt a dreame to night.
Mer. And fo did I.
Ro. Well what was yours?
Mer. That dreamers often lie.
Ro. In bed afleep while they do dream things true.
Mer. O then I fee Queene Mab hath bin with you:
She is the Fairies midwife,and fhe comes in fhape no bigger the
an Agot ftone, on the forefinger of an Alderman, drawne with
a teeme of little ottamie.ouer mens nofes as they lie afleep: her
waggo fpokes made of lög fpi rs legs:the couer,of the wings
of Grafhoppers,her traces of the fmalleft fpider web,her collors
of the moonfhines watry beams,her whip of Crickets bone,the
lafh of Philome,her waggoner, a fmall grey coated Gnat, not
half fo big as a round litle worme,prickt from the lazie finger of
a man.Her Charriot is an emptie Hafel nut,Made by the Ioyner
fquirrel or old Grub,time out amind,the Fairie, Coatchmakers:
and in this ftate fhe gallops nightby night, throgh louers brains,
and then they dreame of loue.On Courtiers knees,that dreame
on Curfies ftrait ore Lawyers fingers who ftrait dreame on fees,
ore Ladies lips who ftrait one kiffes dream, which oft the angrie
Mab with blifters plagues , becaufe their breath with fweete
meate tainted are. Sometime fhe gallops ore a Courtiers nofe,
and then dreames he of fmelling out a fute:and fometime comes
fhe with a tithpigs taile,tickling a Perfons nofe as a hes afleepe,
then he dreames of an other Benefice. Sometime fhe driueth ore
a fouldiers neck,and then dreames he of cutting forrain throates,
of breaches,ambufcados,fpanifh blades:Of healths fiue fadome
deepe , and then anon drums in his eare,at which he ftartes and
wakes,and being thus frighted, fweares a praier or two & fleeps
againe:this is that very Mab that plats the manes of hoifes in the
night : and bakes the Elklocks in foule fluttifh haires, which
once vntangled,much misfortune bodes.
                                                   C 2   This

Mr. WILLIAM
SHAKESPEARES

COMEDIES,
HISTORIES, &
TRAGEDIES.

Published according to the True Originall Copies.

Martin Droeshout sculpsit London.

LONDON

Printed by Isaac Iaggard, and Ed. Blount. 1623.

Opposite page: Title page of the First Folio. As the inscription in the upper right corner indicates, this copy of the book was a gift to its first owner, the Herald Augustine Vincent, from the printer, "William Jaggard Typographi," in 1623.
This page: A rare "proof sheet" of the First Folio, with the proofreader's marks pointing to typographical errors in the setting of ANTHONY AND CLEOPATRA.

first time include some of the relatively less popular—*Cymbeline, Timon of Athens, All's Well That Ends Well*—but also a number of the best loved: *Julius Caesar, Macbeth, Twelfth Night, The Tempest.* That Shakespeare went to his grave not knowing, and possibly not caring, whether works so inestimably valued by future generations would survive has puzzled many and given a perhaps unintended point to Matthew Arnold's celebrated sonnet:

> Others abide our question. Thou art free.
> We ask and ask—Thou smilest and art still,
> Out-topping knowledge.

Had not Shakespeare over and over again proclaimed, in his own Sonnets, the power of his art to eternize his subject? In the first quatrain of Sonnet 55, the poet thus addresses his adored Fair Youth:

> Not marble nor the gilded monuments
> Of princes shall outlive this pow'rful rhyme;
> But you shall shine more bright in these contents
> Than unswept stone, besmear'd with sluttish time.

But the poet speaks in this fashion only in his non-dramatic verse. The plays which Shakespeare gave to his company found their fullest realization not in the privacy of the reader's study, but in performance on the boards by actors for the applause of audiences experiencing the unique communal magic of live theatre. It therefore seems fitting that actors published the plays which Shakespeare, player and playwright, created for them.

Of all the glories of the age that saw Drake circumnavigate the globe and a small island withstand the might of Spain, a single book stands out as the paramount glory. Let Ben Jonson, who contributed to it the noblest commemorative poem in the language, have the last word:

> Thou art a monument without a tomb,
> And art alive still while thy book doth live,
> And we have wits to read, and praise to give.

Epilogue

To what blest genius of the isle,
Shall Gratitude her tribute pay,
Decree the festive day,
Erect the statue, and devote the pile?

Do not your sympathetic hearts accord,
To own the "bosom's lord?"
'Tis he! 'tis he!—that demi-god!
Who Avon's flow'ry margin trod,
While sportive *Fancy* round him flew,
Where *Nature* led him by the hand,
Instructed him in all she knew,
And gave him absolute command!
'Tis he! 'tis he!
"The god of our idolatry!"

From David Garrick's "Ode upon Dedicating a Building, and Erecting a Statue, to Shakespeare, at Stratford upon Avon, 1769."

As Shakespeare's popularity increased during the latter half of the eighteenth century and the first half of the nineteenth century, his presence was felt in the visual and plastic arts. Particularly in evidence were Shakespearean ceramic figurines, illustrated here by (a) a Derby porcelain of Falstaff, (b) a Staffordshire bust of Shakespeare, (c) a Staffordshire pottery replica of a Shakespeare clock, (d) a white stoneware copy (attributed to Enoch Wood) of the Shakespeare memorial statue by Peter Scheemakers in Westminster Abbey, and (e) a Staffordshire pottery rendering of John Philip Kemble as Hamlet.

A remarkable thing happens on the way to the Forum in *Julius Caesar.* During the ritual of the bloodbath following Caesar's assassination, Cassius and Brutus reflect on how in future ages—"in states unborn and accents yet unknown"—players will perform these portentous events for the amusement of theatre audiences. Thus, in the midst of one of the most solemn moments of his drama, does Shakespeare challenge the dramatic illusion itself, reminding us that we are, after all, only watching a play. But for the generations after Shakepeare's mortal remains were gathered up for burial in Holy Trinity Church, the special *frisson* of this moment in *Julius Caesar* would have been unavailable had the play not been included within the covers of the First Folio. The publication of that volume represents not only the climax of the English Renaissance but also the prelude to three and a half centuries of performance, exegesis, and criticism.

Three more Folios followed in the seventeenth century: the Second in 1632; the Third in 1663, to the second impression of which, in 1664, were added "seven plays, never before printed in Folio," including *Pericles;* and, finally, the Fourth in 1685, a bulkier volume than its predecessors. The Third Folio additions—mostly apocryphal plays, such as *The London Prodigal,* which capitalized on Shakespeare's popularity—displaced the Droeshout engraving from title page to frontispiece position. Successive reprintings took their toll on the portrait. In an attempt to freshen up the worn plate, crosshatching was added to much of the surface. As a result, the Shakespeare who peers out at readers from the last Folio boasts a chin covered with stubble, as well as oily highlights on the face. He needs a wash and a shave. It was time for a new edition.

This was supplied early in the next century by Nicholas Rowe, himself a dramatist and poet—eventually, in 1715, Poet Laureate. Rowe catered to changing tastes. Instead of a single massive volume, he offered six convenient small ones in his 1709 edition. He modernized spelling and punctuation, emended some doubtful or puzzling readings, and divided the plays into acts and scenes. He provided a convenient cast list preceding each play, and included a general introduction, illustrations especially commissioned for the occasion, and a scattering of notes. In this fashion Rowe launched the modern Shakespearean editorial tradition. There followed an apostolic succession of eighteenth-century editors. Among these pioneers were Samuel Johnson, whose introduction to Shakepeare's works is itself a literary classic, and Edmond Malone, whose labors on the text, the chronology of the plays, Elizabethan stage history, and Shakespeare's biography have earned him the esteem of posterity as the greatest of Shakespeare scholars.

As early as 1634, a Lieutenant Hammond had visited Stratford, and in Holy Trinity Church taken note of the "neat monument of that famous English poet, Mr. William Shakespeare, who was born there." Other tourists followed, first in a trickle, then in a steady stream, and finally in a deluge. Gradually, as Shakespeare's plays were reprinted and revived, a broad public came to realize that the popular playwright of the Elizabethan stage was also the supreme genius of English letters. Before the end of the eighteenth century, Shakespeare worship—the phenomenon we call Bardolatry—had come into being. The glover's son reigned as undisputed monarch of literature.

The public coronation took place in Stratford during three days in September of 1769. Bells rang for the Shakespeare Jubilee; cannons roared, fireworks lit up the sky, and serenaders sang Shakespeare's praises. In Holy Trinity the bust was decked with flowers. The premier actor of the day, David Garrick, presided over the festivities and delivered the Jubilee oration, concluding with the line, "we shall not look upon his like again." Tumultuous applause followed the speech. Also driving rains, which flooded the octagonal wooden amphitheatre erected for the occasion on the Avon's bank. The celebrants almost literally drifted away. No matter. Garrick's Jubilee had enthroned Shakespeare as National Poet and culture hero. "And when Willy sung, all the Deities swore / They ne'er heard such warbling, such wild notes before," an anonymous rhymester rhapsodized two years later in the *Universal Magazine:*

> Let Britons, inraptur'd, their thanks swell on high,
> One Shakespeare on earth—one Jove in the sky.

Shakespeare was on his way to becoming (in James Joyce's

FALSTAFF, an ink and watercolor sketch (ca. 1858) by George Cruikshank.

phrase) "the playwright who wrote the Folio of the world."

A mystique so overpowering in its appeal invites heresy. As early as the eighteenth century, a few skeptics began to express muted doubts about the recipient of veneration. How could the god of popular idolatry be also vulnerable flesh and blood? Could that supremely intelligent being have been born to illiterate parents in backwater Stratford, reared with yokels in a bookless neighborhood, and then gone on to write *Hamlet* and the rest? Heads shook gravely. In the fullness of time, alternative candidates were offered, preferably candidates with university degrees and blue blood coursing through their veins.

Perhaps the most famous of the disbelievers is Delia Bacon. Born in 1811 in a log cabin in Ohio, Delia migrated to England, where she pursued investigations designed to unmask the Stratford Impostor and reveal the true author, who, by a curious coincidence, bore her surname. Delia's strategy included an assault on the poet's grave. With candle in one hand and lantern in the other, she slipped into Holy Trinity Church by night and measured the crevices on either side of the gravestone before fleeing, her mission unaccomplished. In 1857 she published *The Philosophy of the Plays of Shakspere Unfolded.* Two years later, incoherent and mad, she died—but not without first having claimed her descent from Francis Bacon. Other dissidents have since championed Bacon, or argued for one earl or another: Oxford, or Derby, or Rutland—almost any earl will do. These anti-Stratfordian theories do not agitate the great majority of readers or playgoers, or those professionally concerned with Shakespeare and his times. As children of a democracy, we do not need to be persuaded of the potentialities for literary accomplishment in plebeian citizens—even the offspring of unlettered immigrants. The Shakespeare documents all cohere in attesting to his authorship of the plays and poems that go by his name.

Visitors to Stratford continue to pause before the monument in Holy Trinity, and to file through the Birthplace in Henley Street. New editions of Shakespeare issue unceasingly from the presses. Translations proliferate. On the stage, and more lately on television, the plays ever renew themselves in performance. Shakespeare lives.

The Shakespeare cult in England reached its eighteenth-century apogee with David Garrick (1717–1779), foremost actor of his age, who not only acted in and produced Shakespearean plays but also helped organize the first Shakespeare celebration, the Shakespeare Jubilee, at Stratford-upon-Avon during the week of September 6, 1769. One object that reminds us of the esteem in which Garrick was held is the ornate loving cup (opposite page) commemorating his accomplishments as a Shakespearean actor: As the watercolor drawing 1, the J.S. Miller engraving of Garrick and Shakespeare 2, and the admission ticket 3 should make clear, the Jubilee attracted large crowds who wished to do honor to the playwright and to the actor who had brought his works to life through distinguished portrayals of such roles as Richard III 4, here captured in a colored 1798 Thomas Cook engraving from an earlier painting by William Hogarth. The highlight of the Jubilee was Garrick's recitation 5 of an "Ode upon Dedicating a Building, and Erecting a Statue, to Shakespeare." Other indications of Garrick's prominence as a Shakespearean are 6 an engraving of Joshua Reynolds's painting of GARRICK BETWEEN TRAGEDY AND COMEDY, with impressions of Garrick's Shakespeare seal, and 7 an enamel medallion presented to Garrick by his fellow actors at Drury Lane in 1777.

Like the Garrick loving cup shown on page 184, the small statuette and ink stand shown here **1** were reputedly carved from the wood of Shakespeare's mulberry tree. But Bardolatry is a twentieth-century phenomenon too, as illustrated by **2** a limited edition Royal Doulton Shakespeare jug produced ca. 1916. Also characteristic of Shakespeare kitsch **3** are a set of silver forks with Shakespearean characters on the handles and a whale's tooth with a scrimshaw portrait of Shakespeare. Even major painters like George Romney succumbed to Bardolatry in the eighteenth century, as illustrated below **4** by

Romney's allegorical oil painting, THE INFANT SHAKESPEARE ATTENDED BY NATURE AND THE PASSIONS. This was one of two Romney oils commissioned by John Boydell for his Shakespeare Gallery, where more than 150 paintings of Shakespearean scenes and characters were exhibited between 1789 and 1804. An elephant folio of engravings from the paintings was published in 1803. In THE AMERICAN EDITION OF BOYDELL'S ILLUSTRATIONS OF THE DRAMATIC WORKS OF SHAKESPEARE (New York, 1852), Romney's INFANT SHAKESPEARE was described as follows: "In this allegorical composi-

tion, Nature is represented as having withdrawn the veil from her countenance in complaisance to her favorite child, who is seated between Joy and Sorrow. On the right hand of Nature are seen Love, Hatred, and Jealousy; on her left appear Anger, Envy, and Fear. In the air are seen the Spirits, startled at the birth of a being so extraordinary." George Cruikshank's nineteenth-century rendering of the same blessed event **5**, THE FIRST APPEARANCE OF WILLIAM SHAKESPEARE ON THE STAGE OF "THE GLOBE"—WITH PART OF HIS DRAMATIC COMPANY— IN 1564, is less solemn—respectful of the

subject matter but lightened by Cruikshank's tendency toward caricature. But there is nothing detached and light-hearted in the writings of Delia Bacon, here illustrated by a letter to Nathaniel Hawthorne **6** proposing Francis Bacon as the true author of the works attributed to Shakespeare. Hawthorne's reply **7** is polite but noncommittal. Delia's crusade did prompt other responses, however, such as the two turn-of-the-century cartoons by **8** Joseph Clayton Clarke and **9** Max Beerbohm (from THE POET'S CORNER, London, 1904), the latter entitled "Shakespeare, His Method of Work."

8

5

9

1

2

3

5

MR MARSTON as MACDUFF.
London Published by J.REDINGTON, Prince Street...

4

MISS O'NEIL as JULIET.
Published by J.Bailey...Inn Lane Holborn, London.

6

7

Over the years, Shakespeare and his plays have inspired hundreds of drawings, paintings, engravings, and other works of visual art. Among the more interesting ones are several shown here: **1** Pamela Coleman Smith's CALIBAN, a watercolor dating from ca. 1900; **2** Juan Carlos Liberti's lithograph of Hamlet from a 1976 Spanish edition of HAMLET; **3** Arthur Rackham's watercolor and ink painting of a mermaid on a dolphin's back, from an illus-

trated 1908 edition of *A MIDSUMMER
NIGHT'S DREAM;* **4–6** *three early-
nineteenth-century tinsel prints of
prominent performers playing such
roles as Macduff, Romeo, and Juliet;
and* **7** *a Thomas Rowlandson water-
color-and-ink painting (ca. 1790) of a
backstage view of a late eighteenth-
century MACBETH performance.
Among the best known of Henry
Fuseli's many Shakespearean paintings
is an oil rendering* **8** *of ARIEL, ca. 1800.*

8

1

3

5

Shakespeare remains the most frequently performed playwright in most of the countries of the world, and his plays and their offshoots are treated in an unending variety of ways. Shown here are: **1** Natalie Wood and Richard Beymer in the 1961 film version of WEST SIDE STORY (directed by Robert Wise and Jerome Robbins), **2** a 1975 Slovak National Theatre production of KING LEAR, **3** a 1978 Bucharest National Theatre production of MACBETH, **4** a 1979 Stockholm City Theatre production of OTHELLO, **5** a 1978 San Francisco American Conservatory Theatre production of THE WINTER'S TALE, **6** a 1978 Munich Kammerspiele production of A MIDSUMMER NIGHT'S DREAM, and **7** a 1976 Stratford Festival Canada production of A MIDSUMMER NIGHT'S DREAM (featuring Jessica Tandy and Hume Cronyn).

Costume designers are among the most creative interpreters of Shakespeare. Fanny Kemble's costumes in the nineteenth century were painted on transparent mica, with the face left blank to allow a picture of the actress's own face to be seen through the mica. The sketch shown here **1** dates from ca. 1830. For one of the most memorable Othello performances in American theatre history, Robert E. Jones designed the Paul Robeson costume **2** audiences saw in 1943. Douglas A. Russell of the Yale School of the Drama designed the costumes for the Three Witches **3** for a production of MACBETH in 1961. And Bjorn Wiinblad designed a dazzling costume for Prospero **4** in the Dallas Theater Center's 1965 production of THE TEMPEST. But seldom have there been costumes to match those designed by Salvador Dali for a 1948 production of AS YOU LIKE IT. One ("Vaneur") is shown below.

*Shakespeare has been performed in a
stunning variety of languages and cul-
tural settings. Shown here are* **1** *a pro-
gram for a 1979 Shanghai Youth
Theatre production of MUCH ADO
ABOUT NOTHING in China,* **2** *a 1955
Parisian poster for a performance of
Hector Berlioz's opera ROMEO ET
JULIETTE,* **3** *a 1979 Belgian poster for
a production of MACBETH,* **4** *a 1936
Netherlands poster for a production of*

A MIDSUMMER NIGHT'S DREAM, 5 a 1937 Greek poster for a production of HAMLET, 6 a 1933 U.S.S.R. program for a Moscow performance of HAMLET, 7 a 1978 Czechoslovakian poster for a production of THE TAMING OF THE SHREW, 8 a 1975 French playbill for a production of RICHARD II, and 9 a 1903 playbill for a Japanese production of OTHELLO.

How Shakespeare "looks" on today's stage depends in large measure on how the director, the set designer, and the costume designer choose to translate the playwright's work into a modern idiom. Shown at left is a moment from the celebrated Peter Brook production of A MIDSUMMER NIGHT'S DREAM, in which a stark white set forms the background for only a few properties, such as the bright red feather which serves as Titania's bower (Royal Shakespeare Company at Stratford-upon-Avon, 1970). Also modern, but much different in approach, is the Richard L. Hay set design (right) for a 1974 Angus Bowmer Theater production of TWO GENTLEMEN OF VERONA at the Oregon Shakespearean Festival in Ashland.

Shakespeare's omnipresence in the modern world is manifested in many fascinating ways, ranging from performances and translations in such languages as 1 Japanese, 2 German, and 3 Swahili, to productions in settings as diverse as 4 eighteenth-century Baltimore, 5 a World War I German prison camp, and 6 Gay Nineties San Francisco. Also illustrative are 7 a special tercentenary issue of THE THEATRE magazine in 1916, 8 A 1978 Mark Antony costume design from the Missouri Repertory Company in Kansas City, 9 a 1977 poster from Stratford Festival Canada in Ontario, 10 a playbill on ship's canvas for an 1853 Arctic production aboard the HMS Resolute, 11 a nineteenth-century London engraving of "Park's Shakespeare Characters," 12, 13 political adaptations lampooning Lyndon Johnson and Richard Nixon, 14 a HAMLET comic book, 15 a devotional calendar for readers of Shakespeare and the Bible, 16 ornate bindings of an 1824 collection of Shakespeare portraits and a 1916 edition of the poet's Songs and Sonnets, alongside an eighteenth-century basalt bust of the Bard, 17 a Bardolaters' poker cloth, 18 a home companion to simplify Shakespeare for the everyday consumer, 19 a nineteenth-century caricature of John Philip Kemble's Hamlet, 20 a cartoon from an anthology, SHAKESPEARE FOR THE BIRDS, 21 a drag parody of the Balcony Scene in ROMEO AND JULIET, 22 a French lottery poster, 23 a drawing of sophisticated New York playgoers in the Twenties, and 24 a May 1979 NEW YORKER magazine cartoon.

"Philosopher, playwright, knower of men, colleague, pal o' mine."

SHAKESPEARE. Louis Francois Roubiliac's terra cotta model, ca. 1757, for the marble statue of Shakespeare he executed for David Garrick's Shakespeare Temple in Hampton. (The marble statue is now in the British Museum.)

The poet's eye, in a fine frenzy rolling
Doth glance from heaven to earth, from earth to heaven;
And as imagination bodies forth
The forms of things unknown, the poet's pen
Turns them to shapes, and gives to airy nothing
A local habitation and a name.
Such tricks hath strong imagination....

Select Reading List

Akrigg, G. P. V. *Jacobean Pageant, or The Court of King James I.* Cambridge, Mass., 1962.

Ashley, Maurice. *England in the Seventeenth Century.* The Pelican History of England, Vol. 6; Harmondsworth, Eng., 1952.

Barbour, Philip L. *Pocahontas and Her World.* Boston, 1969.

Bindoff, S. T. *Tudor England.* The Pelican History of England, Vol. 5. Harmondsworth, Eng., 1950.

Dunlop, Ian. *Palaces & Progresses of Elizabeth I.* London, 1962.

Eccles, Mark. *Shakespeare in Warwickshire.* Madison, Wis., 1961.

Fordham, Herbert George. *Some Notable Surveyors & Map-Makers of the Sixteenth, Seventeenth, & Eighteenth Centuries and Their Work: A Study in the History of Cartography.* Cambridge, 1929.

Fox, Levi. *The Borough Town of Stratford-upon-Avon.* The Corporation of Stratford-upon-Avon, 1953.

Fraser, Antonia. *King James VI of Scotland, I of England.* London, 1974.

Greenblatt, Stephen J. *Sir Walter Ralegh: The Renaissance Man and His Roles.* New Haven and London, 1973.

Gurr, Andrew. *The Shakespearean Stage, 1574–1642.* Cambridge, 1970.

Harting, James Edmund. *The Birds of Shakespeare.* Chicago, 1965. (Reprint, with an Introduction by Grundy Steiner, of *The Ornithology of Shakespeare Critically Examined, Explained, and Illustrated* [London, 1871].)

Lacey, Robert. *Sir Walter Ralegh.* London, 1973.

Laslett, Peter. *The World We Have Lost.* London, 1965; 2nd ed., 1971.

Lyman, Edward. *British Maps and Map-Makers.* London, 1947.

Mattingly, Garrett. *The Armada.* Boston, 1959.

Morison, Samuel Eliot. *The European Discovery of America: The Northern Voyages A.D. 500–1600.* New York, 1971.

——. *The European Discovery of America: The Southern Voyages A.D. 1492–1616.* New York, 1974.

Neale, J. E. *Queen Elizabeth.* London, 1934.

A New Companion to Shakespeare Studies. Eds. Kenneth Muir and S. Schoenbaum. Cambridge, 1971.

Ordish, Thomas Fairman. *Shakespeare's London.* New ed.; London, 1904.

Painter, George D. *William Caxton: A Quincentenary Biography of England's First Printer.* London, 1976.

Phipson, Emma. *The Animal-Lore of Shakespeare's Time.* London, 1883.

Rohde, Eleanour Sinclair. *Shakespeare's Wild Flowers: Fairy Lore, Gardens, Nests, Gatherers of Simples, and Bee Lore.* London: The Medici Society, 1935.

Rowse, A. L. *The England of Elizabeth: The Structure of Society.* London, 1950.

——. *William Shakespeare: A Biography.* London, 1963.

Schoenbaum, S. *William Shakespeare: A Compact Documentary Life.* New York, 1977.

Seager, H. W. *Natural History in Shakespeare's Time.* London, 1896.

Shakespeare's England: An Account of the Life & Manners of His Age. 2 vols. Oxford, 1916. (Contains chapters on religion, commerce and coinage, law, costume, sports and pastimes, etc.)

Smith, Lacey Baldwin. *Elizabeth Tudor: Portrait of a Queen.* Boston, 1975.

——. *The Horizon Book of the Elizabethan World.* New York, 1967.

Stephenson, Henry. *Shakespeare's London.* New York, 1905.

Williams, Neville. *All the Queen's Men: Elizabeth I and Her Courtiers.* London, 1972.

——. *The Royal Residences of Great Britain.* London, 1960.

Index

F

G

H

W-Z

T

U

V

Illustration Acknowledgments

Unless otherwise indicated, all illustrations included in this book derive from material in the collections of the Folger Shakespeare Library in Washington, D.C. Photography at the Folger was executed by or supervised by Horace Groves, head photographer, with the assistance of Robert Jackson. Other photography is credited below.

p. 2 (frontispiece) by Rudy Muller
p. 6 by Betsy K. Frampton
p. 146 by Rudy Muller
p. 148 by Leslie Spatt
p. 150, no. 12, by Hannes Killian
p. 151, no. 15, courtesy Museum of Modern Art Film Archive
no. 16, copyright © 1960 by Playbill, Inc.
p. 163, no. 12, by Martha Swope, courtesy American Shakespeare Theatre
no. 17, copyright © 1976 by Paul Davis
p. 166, no. 12, courtesy Harvard Theatre Collection
no. 16, courtesy Museum of Modern Art Film Archive
p. 180 by Rudy Muller
p. 184 by Rudy Muller
p. 185, no. 7, by Rudy Muller
p. 186, nos. 1, 2, 3, by Rudy Muller
p. 190, no. 1, courtesy Museum of Modern Art Film Archive
no. 2, by Joset Vavro, courtesy Slovak National Theatre, Bratislava, Czechoslovakia
no. 3, by Adelheid Lorenz, courtesy Stadtische Theatre, Karl-Marx-Stadt, East Germany
no. 4, by Andre Lafolie, courtesy Stockholm City Theatre, Sweden
no. 5, by William Ganslen, courtesy American Conservatory Theatre, San Francisco
no. 6, by Max Sayle, courtesy Kammerspiele, Munich, West Germany
p. 191 by Robert C. Ragsdale, courtesy Stratford Festival Canada, Stratford, Ontario
p. 192, no. 2, gift of James O. Belden in memory of Evelyn Berry Belden
p. 196 courtesy Holte Photographics Ltd., Stratford-upon-Avon
p. 197 by Hank Kranzler, courtesy Oregon Shakespearean Festival, Ashland
p. 199, no. 20, copyright © 1974 by Darian Olson
p. 200 by Rudy Muller